Acting
Year One

Rodney B. Whatley
Pensacola State College

Long Grove, Illinois

For information about this book, contact:
Waveland Press, Inc.
4180 IL Route 83, Suite 101
Long Grove, IL 60047-9580
(847) 634-0081
info@waveland.com
www.waveland.com

Photo on page viii courtesy of Xiaolun Chen. All other photos © Pensacola State College and used with permission.

Copyright © 2023 by Waveland Press, Inc.

10-digit ISBN 1-4786-4878-3
13-digit ISBN 978-1-4786-4878-9

All rights reserved. No part of this book may be reproduced, stored in a retrieval system, or transmitted in any form or by any means without permission in writing from the publisher.

Printed in the United States of America

7 6 5 4 3 2 1

Contents

Acknowledgments vii
About the Author viii

Introduction 1

Lesson 1
Introduction to Class 3

Lesson 2
Warm-Up Exercises 12

Lesson 3
Monologue #1 Rehearsal 17

Lesson 4
Monologue #1 Performance Day 22

Lesson 5
The Voice and the Face: It's All in Your Head 24

Lesson 6
Cold-Reading Audition: Iceberg, Right Ahead! 37

Lesson 7
Script Analysis: And How Does That Make You Feel? 43

Lesson 8
The Body: I Like to Move It, Move It 56

Lesson 9
The Mind—Changing Yours 69

Lesson 10
The Soul—That's the Spirit! **82**

Lesson 11
Audition Technique: How to Do That Thing You Do **94**

Lesson 12
Stage Fright—Boo! **106**

Lesson 13
Monologue #2 Rehearsal: Tragic or Serious Monologue **113**

Lesson 14
Day Two Monologue #2 Rehearsal:
Tragic or Serious Monologue **116**

Lesson 15
Performance Day Monologue #2:
Tragic or Serious Monologue **118**

Lesson 16
Hard Work: If You Can Get It **120**

Lesson 17
The Difference Between Tragic and Comedic Acting **134**

Lesson 18
Monologue #3 Rehearsal **151**

Lesson 19
Day Two Monologue #3 Rehearsal **152**

Lesson 20
Monologue #3 Performance **154**

Lesson 21
Working with Others: Everybody Farts **155**

Lesson 22
Blocking a Scene: No, Stage Right. The Other Stage Right! **171**

Lesson 23
Repetition and the Illusion of the First Time:
Band Name or Chapter Title?   **185**

Lesson 24
Scene #1 Rehearsal   **195**

Lesson 25
Day Two Scene #1 Rehearsal   **196**

Lesson 26
Day Three Scene #1 Rehearsal   **197**

Lesson 27
Scene #1 Performance   **198**

Lesson 28
Scene #2 Rehearsal   **200**

Lesson 29
Day Two Scene #2 Rehearsal   **201**

Lesson 30
Day Three Scene #2 Rehearsal   **202**

Lesson 31
Final Exam: Scene #2 Performance   **204**

Conclusion   **205**

Works Cited   **209**
Index   **211**

Acknowledgments

I would like to acknowledge Robert Gandrup for the sets and the technical direction; Lavonne French for the costumes; Carrie Whatley for everything; and everyone at Pensacola State College and the theatre community in the greater Pensacola, Florida, area.

About the Author

Rodney Whatley has a BFA in Theatre from University of Montevallo, an MFA in Theatre from Lindenwood University, and a PhD in Dramatic Theory and Criticism from Florida State University. He has previously published a book entitled *Mametspeak*. Dr. Whatley taught his first class in 1994. In 2005, he became Director of Theatre at Pensacola State College, where he teaches Acting I, Acting II, Directing I, Dramatic Literature, and other theatre classes. Dr. Whatley lives in Florida with his wife, Carrie, and their four fur babies: Jack, Doogie Bowser, Jonny, and Princess. They hope to rescue more dogs in the future.

Dr. Rodney Whatley

Introduction

Reader, this is the book; book, this is the reader. There—introductions are done.

The purpose of this book is twofold: first, the book is meant to teach students how to act. The voice of the book speaks to them. Secondly, the book is intended as a guide for professors teaching Acting I in the college and university setting. Its structure and content serve as a lesson plan and guidebook for the teaching of Acting I.

The book follows the schedule I teach: a standard sixteen-week semester, with two class meetings per week. I usually teach either a Monday-Wednesday, or a Tuesday-Thursday schedule, with each class day lasting one hour and fifteen minutes. The lessons are divided into that schedule; however, with some craftiness, the lessons can be adapted to other schedules, so teachers should not feel that if their classes do not meet this number of days or for this amount of time, that this book cannot help them. I believe it is easily adaptable to other schedules, even if a little elbow grease might be called upon to squeeze it into those square holes.

As I said, the voice of the book speaks primarily to the students in the classroom. It is highly recommended that the students read each chapter before the associated lessons because some of the lessons contain more theory than can be discussed or lectured about in an hour and fifteen minutes, and who wants to listen to lectures anyway? The exercises for each class can be performed within the class time to explicate the theory through practice. These are exercises that I have created over the years, and if the professor or teacher does not like them, they can substitute with their own. I just thought these were effective at showcasing the practice behind the theory, providing examples that show ideas in action.

I have included grade sheets for each acting assignment in the book as well, as it is my philosophy that it is good to let students know how they are going to be graded in advance, so that the assignment is not such an anxiety-generating mystery. I created these grade sheets over the years for my class and they are intended merely as suggestions. The professor or teacher can substitute with their preferred grade sheets or with those they have personally created for their own classes. My evaluation sheets continue to evolve as I teach the class each semester.

The research concept driving this book was to avoid a dry treatise on acting that included input from every expert on acting who ever lived. Rather, this is intended as a practical book for the teaching and learning of acting; therefore, I read actors' autobiographies and included the most relevant as source material. In addition to relevant autobiographies, I also included a couple of indispensable biographies.

Disclaimer: acting is not a science. This book contains ideas about acting, but they are, in the end, only opinions about acting. No one knows everything, but my desire is to share some of the things I have been taught. Please turn off all cell phones and electronic devices and enjoy the show.

Lesson 1
Introduction to Class

What is acting? The problem with trying to define acting is that, since it is an art, it can mean different things to different people. Because of that, there are many acting books and disciplines that contradict each other as to the true nature of acting. Can we know what acting is? Maybe. Alec Baldwin (2017) wrote, "There is a saying in show business, 'No one knows anything,' an attempt to convey the inscrutability of show business and particularly the key to success" (204). So not even Alec Baldwin can definitively say what acting is. We will have to determine the definition of acting for ourselves.

Hello, Dolly!

> **Exercise 1**
> 1. Break the class into discussion groups.
> 2. Each group discusses and formulates a response that defines acting. Write the definition out so the exact wording can be used to share your conception with the rest of the class.
> 3. Each group shares their results with the rest of the class.
> 4. The class examines all responses and discusses conceptions of the definition of acting.

The thesis behind this book and my theory of acting is that great acting comes from a concerted effort of the actor's entire instrument. The actor's instrument is everything the actor possesses. As Sissy Spacek (2012) describes it, "Little did I know . . . that my skills as a twirler with the marching band would come in handy with my first starring role. Or that every experience, every story I heard as a child, every person who crossed my path, was like a gift that I would carry with me for the rest of my life" (2). An actor's resource pool is everything that constitutes that actor.

Constituting the actor is a trinity of qualities: the mind, the body, and the soul. For great acting to occur, all three areas must be fully engaged. Three is a magic number, so all three areas need to be engaged to create the magic of theatre. Shawn Levy (2014), in discussing Robert De Niro's preparation for *Taxi Driver,* touches on the concept of the acting trinity: "This was a role that had to be built of the raw material of his imagination, his body, and his soul" (166). His concept of the imagination is synonymous with my concept of the actor's mind; here we have imagination's source, the mind, along with the body and the soul. Levy (2014) also quoted Shelley Winters as saying to a young De Niro while filming the Roger Corman grindhouse classic, *Bloody Mama,* "You have a marvelous *mind, instinct,* and *talent*" (86). The mind in this case is, of course, the mind; instinct is the body, and talent is the soul.

It takes total dedication and immersion to be good at acting, or as Alan Arkin (2011) says, "Acting can be anything one wants it to be, from the most crass, dead, ego-driven activity, used as a way of earning an easy living or finding women, on the one end, to something sublime, magical, and transforming on the other. And the difference, the only difference, is the investment made by the person who's engaged in the process" (27). The actor is in control of the quality of their acting. Actors get out of acting what they put in. Some of what actors need to put into their acting include:

1. Willingness to read scripts
2. Willingness to read scripts aloud, either alone or with other actor artists

3. Willingness to understand and accept an artist's responsibilities
4. Willingness to memorize lines for however long it takes
5. Willingness to put electronic distractions away while memorizing lines
6. Willingness to rehearse outside of class or rehearsal
7. Willingness to receive positive and negative feedback
8. Willingness to actively support the work of classmates
9. Willingness to change, evolve, and grow

In this class, from this day forward, you are no longer just classmates, but castmates. Signing up for this class is the equivalent of being cast in a repertory company in which you will perform a scene of reader's theatre, three monologues, and two scenes. In the comic strip *Peanuts,* Lucy once asked Charlie Brown, "Why are we here?" She of course meant, "Why are human beings are on Earth? What is our great human purpose?" Charlie Brown responded, "We are here to make others happy." In that vein, you are here to make sure your classmate castmates succeed. Their success is your success. Their success is your responsibility. The good news is that you also now have all your classmates pulling for you and supporting your success.

There are many different character types and many different theatrical styles, expanding outwards from non-realism to realism as the two opposite poles on the spectrum, but the majority of acting, and thus the focus of an Acting I class, is actors playing people. You are a person pretending to be another person. Therefore, the goal of much of acting can be considered the same, and that is for the audience to believe that the actor, who is lying, is actually telling the truth. Or, as Gene Wilder (2005) puts it when he answers the question of what actors want: "I think to be *believed*—onstage or on-screen—is the one hope that all actors share. Which one of us, anywhere in the world, doesn't yearn to be believed when the audience is watching?" (56).

Alec Baldwin (2017) cites a lesson learned from a costar in soap operas. "O'Brien would tell me acting is about making the audience believe what I'm saying" (58). Part of being a good actor comes down to convincing friends and strangers that you are sincere in what you are saying and doing. In Ancient Greece, actors were called *hypokrites*, which evolved into the English language word "hypocrite," because *hypokrites* did not mean what they said—they were insincere, doing their best to fake sincerity.

It is something that we naturally do in life: tell people in everyday life lies we hope they will believe. Lies like:

- I am 5'10", not 5'8"
- I only weigh 200 pounds
- I am not losing my hair; I get it cut this way
- People who disagree with each other make the best spouses

We lie to people in a way that we hope is believable. One of the ways that we can inspire belief in others is if we believe what we are saying.

How much does an actor need to believe that fiction is truth? It cannot be 100 percent because that entails a loss of the ability to tell the difference between reality and fantasy. Actors believe in a simple way, as simple as the belief of a child when that child is playing pretend. In his novel, *Duma Key*, Stephen King writes about artists and belief. In this case King writes of a painter, but the sentiment applies to performance artists as well. "Art is the concrete artifact of faith and expectation, the realization of a world that would otherwise be little more than a veil of pointless consciousness stretched over a gulf of mystery. And besides—if you don't believe what you see, who will believe your art?" (King 2008, 365). He finishes the section with the pithy statement, "Believing is also *feeling*. Any artist will tell you so" (368).

The actor at work creates a parallel universe, the reality of the stage, separates it from the reality of life, and then invests in the reality of that stage universe. It is the willing suspension of disbelief for the actor. The willing suspension of disbelief is a term of art usually applied to an audience, in that they are willing to believe what they see on the stage is real. To a certain extent, the successful actor must also be willing to believe. What is happening can be true as long as it is in the parallel universe. It is not life, as Alan Arkin (2011) puts it, writing, "Acting is nothing more than a metaphor for life, and a pretty transparent one at that. Theatre is supposed to be an art form, but most of the time it's just life up there" (184–185). The stage universe is a metaphor for life; the actor believes in the metaphor.

Belief opens doorways to many things, such as blocking plans, stage business ideas, and a pathway to genuine emotional reactions in the moment. The ability to convince the audience that your stage lies are truths is integral to your success as an actor. To be clear, let me give some examples of what I mean by stage lies. When I take the stage in a play, I am saying to the audience:

- I am not Rodney Whatley; I am Hamlet.
- I am not in Pensacola, Florida; I am in Denmark.
- It is not 2022; it is the late Middle Ages.
- I am not reciting dialogue from a script; this is the first time I have said these words and I thought of them myself.
- I hate that person; I love that other person.
- I just killed a bunch of people.
- I'm dying. Oops, now I'm dead.
- I am comfortable wearing stage costumes under hot stage lights.

When an actor takes the stage, everything they say and do is fiction, but that art is revealing some truth about the human condition through the artifice. We use these shadows of people to cast light on the human experience.

While the motivations for becoming an actor are many, some are more common than others. Alan Cumming (2014) cites one as the need to escape. "But that day I completely used acting to push away my present, to gain some respite from the chaos and, yes, the fear I knew I'd immediately drop back into when my attention was no longer diverted" (85). Theatre is meant to be a relief to the audience, but it can also serve the same purpose for the actor.

That is a good thing because acting can also be very stressful. It is by nature a competitive art form, designed so from the start through the audition process. It does not stop there, because even once cast, every actor labors under the threat of being replaced by someone better. There is no job security save the director's approval, and who knows what the director wants? Sometimes that even includes the director. Mindy Kaling (2015) puts it this way when discussing the cancellation of her television series by one network, only to then get picked up by another: "I'd gone from barely having time to transition from my panic of not having a job to the panic of more work than I'd ever had before. And that's all show business is, really. Transitioning panics." She concludes that actors "never know what is going to happen" (82–83).

Acting is nerve-wracking and hard work, but there are benefits and rewards. Alan Arkin (2011) said of his time in educational theatre, "I lived for the rehearsals and performances . . . for so many years my sense of comfort and identity was secured only when I was being someone else, but I think this is true of many actors" (16). Part of this comes from the feedback of audiences. When we step onstage, we need to do so with confidence because we are saying to a roomful of people, "Hey! Look at me! Listen to me! What I am saying and doing is

Hello, Dolly!

more important than anything anyone else in this room has to say or do! Quit thinking about food, quit thinking about sex, quit thinking about money, quit thinking about death, quit thinking whatever you are thinking and pay attention to me!"

Gene Wilder (2005) observes of this phenomenon, "When I'm onstage I feel safe. . . . But onstage everyone listens to me and watches me and—if I'm any good—applauds me" (48). And that applause is one of the biggest benefits that an actor can reap. Wilder observes, "Actors are children . . . all we wanted was to be loved for ourselves, just as we were . . . but it didn't seem to be good enough. . . ." He says that as a result we perform for Mama, who calls Daddy to see:

> Mama and Daddy applaud, and they hug us and kiss us and we feel that they really love us, and we grow up longing for that exhilaration again, and we do get it, years later, from an audience that applauds and cheers us and we go home exhilarated and fall asleep feeling loved again, and we need another fix from another audience. I wish I could ... save all those lonely children who become actors and grow up thinking that the applause is actually for them and not for their performance. (241–242)

Audience approval is a powerful drug, and actors should beware of addiction. Pleasing the audience is certainly one actor goal, but there are others.

- You have a duty to the playwright. Honor the intentions of the script.
- You have a duty to directors. Respect their opinions and incorporate them into your work. Students should see the class's professor as their director in an acting class.
- You have a duty to your acting partners. Do your share of the work and do not let them down or disappoint them.

And finally, you have a duty to yourself. As Sidney Poitier (2000) puts it:

> ... for most of my life in films and theater I had believed that an actor should repeatedly seek to have his measure taken by challenges inherent in his craft.
> Every actor should aim always toward earning a place among those privileged members of his profession who are considered by most to be creative, artistic, and suited to their calling. (234)

Keep that in mind this semester when choosing performance material. When it is time to pick a monologue, put forth more of an effort than simply going to a monologue website and picking the first one that pops up. As you rehearse, so will you perform, and as you learn, so will you do.

When choosing monologues or scenes, the best practice is to choose material from plays that have significant value in the dramatic literature canon. If you pick a monologue or scene that is only published on the internet, be sure to closely assess its value. Anybody can publish anything anytime on the internet. What you find self-published on the web may be art, it may be a good choice, but assess its value in furthering your education as a performance artist. Far better it is to choose something that has recognized artistic merit and value that as a professional actor you might be hired to play at some point in your career.

Now is the genesis of your acting career. For a first-year acting class, it is best to pick characters that are near to you or with which you can readily identify. Playing characters that present great challenges and advanced knowledge might be better suited for later in your acting training. Period pieces like Greek plays or Shakespeare, and extremely unrealistic, nonhuman characters, are choices better reserved for advanced acting classes. For instance, Acting II at many colleges and universities customarily consists of scene studies in different styles, specifically Greek, Shakespearean, comic, absurdist, realism, and post-realism, among others.

Hello, Dolly!

In conclusion, acting is an unknowable mystery that requires hard work and dedication, a sacrifice of self-identity, and a complete subjugation of self to the needs of others. The good news is that it is also a lot of fun.

Exercise 2: Introduction Monologue

1. As a class, brainstorm and decide on some key information needed to introduce oneself to a stranger.
2. Each student should then individually take five minutes to create a one-minute monologue of self-introduction.
3. Students will then take turns performing their monologues for the rest of the class.

Exercise 3: Group Bonding

1. The class gathers as a group in a clear space. If weather permits, this exercise should be done outside.
2. Take a beach ball or volleyball. Have someone hit the ball up into the air above the group.
3. The group must keep the ball in the air for at least 100 consecutive hits. The same person may not hit the ball two times in a row. The entire group must participate; there is to be no ball-hogging. The group should count aloud each hit in unison.
4. Failure to reach 100 consecutive hits means you must start the process over.

Exercise 4: Group Bonding II

1. The class forms as a group in a clear space. This can be done either indoors or outdoors. The group forms a circle.
2. The group takes a beach ball or volleyball. The group passes the ball clockwise from person to person. Repeat until quality and ease is achieved. Once this is accomplished, the group passes the ball counterclockwise until quality and ease are achieved. Once this is achieved this exercise is over.
3. One person takes the ball while the group is still in circle formation. That person begins by throwing the ball to a random person in the circle. The catcher then throws the ball to a different random person in the circle. The group continues with random receivers throwing the ball to other people at random. The ball must be thrown always to different people in the circle. Avoid repetition and patterns. Everyone must be equally involved, no ball-hogging.
4. Repeat the exercise from #3 above, only this time without the ball. Use an imaginary ball. Continue the exercise until everyone believes in the ball.

Homework

Your first acting role for this class will be entirely of your own choosing. It is a handshake to the class, an opportunity to make a first impression. It is also the most freedom and latitude you will have for source material all semester. For next class, please bring a printed copy, on paper, of a monologue. It can be from any source, as long as it is dramatized, not narrative. In other words, you will be playing a character, not performing an oral interpretation of a novel or short story in the third person, for example. You must be a character either talking to another character or directly to the audience. This monologue can be from a play, movie, television show, internet video, book, poem, or whatever. The monologue should not exceed sixty seconds, or one minute.

You must bring two printed copies: one for yourself and another for the professor. Bring these copies to class or you will not be able to fully participate in the day's activities. Failure to participate in classroom exercises will detract from your education as well as from your grade.

Lesson 2
Warm-Up Exercises

I must confess that as an actor, I sometimes hated warm-up exercises. Do we really need to do warm-up exercises? Some actors hate them, some love them, I vacillated between the two positions as an actor, but I have come to realize that warm-ups have immense value and should be part of every rehearsal and performance process.

There are the obvious benefits of getting the body and the voice ready for performance. Acting is like dancing or sports—it requires intense physical activity. Stage movement, even in realism, is not the same as movement in life. It takes planning, rehearsal, and intensive concentration. In order to increase effectiveness and reduce the likelihood of injury, physical and vocal warm-ups are necessary.

There is another benefit to warm-ups, in that they also prove to have meditative value. The exercise session can be an airlock to smooth the transition between the hazards of real life and the sanctum of art. Warm-up exercises are an opportunity for the actor to clear their mind and begin to focus on the artistic endeavors into which they are about to launch. You can use warm-ups as a chance to calm yourself and separate yourself from the distractions that can impede you from doing your best work. Your work is a reflection of who you are. By your actions, you create your identity. Your work's quality determines if your contribution to the group will have a positive impact on the group's efforts to improve their community through art, which in turn enhances all human society. The honorable role of artist is a significant burden and deserves respect.

Making the world a better place is all well and good, but the main perk remains your personal benefit, in that warm-ups will improve the quality of your artistic performance. If you do not warm up, then the first portion of your performance, be it a monologue, scene, song, or dance, will serve as the warm-up. Therefore, the first part of your performance, since it is building up to your full potential and is not the actual full potential, will be inferior to the latter part of your performance. While it is important to end with a bang, that bang may be completely ineffectual if it has been defused by a weak beginning. While it is not necessary that every

The Underpants

performance begin with a boom and end with a bang, the start of your piece makes a first impression on the audience. If the first impression is bad enough, it may be too powerful for a great middle and end of a performance to overcome. For these reasons and more, actors should do physical and vocal warm-ups before each rehearsal and performance.

Each class day that contains rehearsals or performances, the class will have warm-up exercises. For each of these exercises, the class will need a leader. A different student will lead exercises each day that requires warming up. In today's class, the professor will lead by example and be the exercise leader, but in the future, student volunteers will lead that day's exercises, both vocal and physical. This is a leadership opportunity. Your classmates' health and well-being are for that day your responsibility.

Exercise 1: Vocals

1. Warming up the lips
2. Warming up the tongue
3. Working the jaw
4. Flexing and relaxing the throat
5. Deep-breathing exercises
6. Tongue-twister exercises
7. Volume variation exercises

Exercise 2: Physicality

1. Stretching the arms
2. Stretching the legs
3. Stretching the torso
4. Make yourself the tallest of the tall, really stretch every portion of your body out. Make yourself the tiniest of the tiny, really scrunch in every aspect of your being, compress yourself into the smallest representation of yourself possible. Make yourself the widest of the wide, spreading yourself as far out in all directions as you can. Make yourself the scrunchiest of the scrunchy, squeezing every molecule of your body as close together as possible.
5. Flex and relax
   A. Lie down on the floor, making sure your body is in alignment.
   B. Beginning at your head, recognize muscles and flex them. Hold the tension for five seconds, then release. Progressively move down your body, recognizing muscles, flexing them, holding the tension for five seconds, then releasing. From head, move to neck, shoulders, biceps, forearms, hands, fingers, chest, stomach, hips, thighs, calves, feet, and toes.
   C. Once complete, repeat, this time starting at your toes and reversing progress back to your head, recognizing muscles, tensing them, holding the tension for five seconds, then releasing.
   D. Once complete, achieve relaxation. Imagine that you are lying on a giant Xerox copy machine. Imagine that the bar of light that travels up and down the document is at the top of your head. As the light bar travels down your body, search for tension, and if you find it, release it. Make sure that the light bar moves slowly, do not rush. When you have reached your toes, run the light bar back up your body to the top of your head to make sure there is no tension. If you are tension-free, rest in total relaxation until the warm-up leader tells you to stand.

Exercise 3: Monologue #1 Work

1. Turn in the professor's copy of your monologue at this time.
2. We are going to dive right into performance. Today each of you will take to the performance space in the room and read your monologue to the class. No sitting; you must stand while delivering your speech. Experience is the best teacher.
3. The first volunteer should take the space.
4. Today the professor will either approve or reject your monologue. If the piece is rejected, you will have to find another. The professor will be happy to assist you in this endeavor if you would like.

5. We will also time your piece to make sure it fits into the sixty-second time limit. If it is too long, it will have to be edited or cut for length. The professor will be happy to assist you in this endeavor if you would like.
6. If the monologue is too short—less than thirty seconds, for example—you will have to add material in order to lengthen it, or choose another, longer monologue to perform. The professor will be happy to assist you in this endeavor if you would like.
7. Upon approval of your monologue, you will need to memorize the piece before the next class.

A Note on Volunteerism

When an acting professor calls for volunteers to get in front of the class and rehearse or perform, it may be tempting to shrink into your chair and look at the floor because you know that if you make eye contact with the professor, they will call on you. This is a symptom of stage fright; do not let it control your education and training.

The Underpants

You are now actors. What do actors do? They act. They do not avoid acting by hiding behind their classmates; they exist to act. Remember: you love acting. Be eager to jump in front of an audience and show off. Performing, not observing, is what you do. You are awesome.

When a teacher calls for volunteers, compete to be the first to perform. If no one volunteers, the teacher will start drafting volunteers. Perhaps you will be the lucky person chosen, especially if you look nervous and terrified.

Homework

The next class session is an off-book rehearsal for all. Come to class with your monologue memorized. Your homework assignment is to memorize your first monologue, Monologue #1. Be able to perform the speech successfully without unwanted pauses, and to do so multiple times. Success can be duplicated. Repeatedly performing the speech without breaks will make the performance better.

There have been times when I thought I had a piece memorized only to find out that I could do it in the car, in the bathroom, or when no one was looking . . . but not in front of an audience. If my superpower is invisibility, but it only works when no one is looking at me, then how do I know I have a superpower? Memorization means the actor can successfully perform the piece in front of other people, an audience, or in this case an audience made up of your classmates.

At times have I wailed in frustration, "I had it this morning, I swear," or "I did it in the car three times today," or "I had this right before class. I don't understand why I can't do it now." It is because I truly did not have it. Do not stop working until you have it, and even then, never stop working until the performance event is completely over, until the performance run is over, and the show is dead, long live the show. In class, actors can continue to work on improving performances until they perform them for a grade and have received their evaluation from the professor.

Lesson 3
Monologue #1 Rehearsal

Today is off-book Monologue #1 rehearsal day. Each student actor will perform their monologue, and after their performance, receive notes as to how they can improve before performing for a grade during the next class session. Next class it is feet-first into the fray once more, dear friends, for the first time.

In this off-book rehearsal you can call for line if you go blank or dry up. That means if you forget something, please say "line" and a designated prompter will cue you as to the oncoming word or phrase in order to get you going again.

No actor forgets lines on purpose, so while it is generous of you to apologize if you forget a line, there is no need to do so. But if you forget that, and apologize, please do not apologize for apologizing. And while memory lapses are frustrating, please refrain from adding expletives to your request for the line. To quote Captain America: "Language!"

Try not to break character or lose intensity; stay in the moment. Be sure to say the request for line loud and clear. Sometimes an actor may whisper, "line." I understand the urge to hide the fact that the actor has lost the words, but the prompter needs to hear your request for the line. Resist the urge to surreptitiously ask for the line.

For those gracious enough to serve as prompter, resist the temptation to watch the performance. Follow along and keep your eyes on the script. It can be a horrible thing for an actor who is sweating bullets due to memory failure to call for line and be met by silence:

>ACTOR: Line!
>
>*(Silence)*
>
>PROMPTER: Oh crap . . . um . . . er . . . sorry.
>
>ACTOR: Sorry.
>
>PROMPTER: No, not sorry. Sorry.
>
>ACTOR: Language! Bad language!
>
>PROMPTER: "Or not to be?"
>
>ACTOR: Or not to be! Dang it, can I start over?

Everyone should serve as a prompter for someone else. At this point, please partner up with a classmate, make a study buddy, and take turns serving as prompter for each other when rehearsal time comes.

Rehearsals are where actors make mistakes, so if you need to start over, just ask. On performance day, however, please avoid starting over if possible, as it is a real momentum killer. It can be like an ice skater who falls but still has to finish the program. An effective rehearsal strategy is to focus on the opening portion of your performance to make sure your grasp of it is solid. In a live theatre performance, actors cannot call for lines and must figure out how to proceed with the scene despite whatever errors occur. It is good to start early by getting into the habit of continuing to perform in spite of mistakes, rather than giving in to them and asking to start over. As you rehearse, so shall you perform.

After each performance in this class, actors will get feedback. Even if your performance is not the one being discussed, every actor can learn from every critique. The notes professors give to one actor may be applicable to the work of everyone else in the class. Do not tune out because your performance isn't the subject of discussion at that moment. The subject under discussion during feedback sessions is always the art of acting. It is not about the actor receiving direct critiques, it is about all of us. For rehearsal performances today, these are the five most pertinent qualities:

1. Energy: Energy includes the actor's enthusiasm to perform. Audiences want to see actors who enjoy performing. If an actor appears miserable onstage, that misery will infect the audience. You are actors. Your purpose is to perform. You love acting! The stage is yours, so take it and do so with pleasure and excited anticipation. While each monologue is different, each demanding its own unique energy signature, the actor must have an appropriate level of energy. Infuse your whole being, all the way to your fingertips, with focused energy. Do not be tired, do not be sleepy, do not be lethargic, and do not be real-life-normal. The stage is not real life, and real-life-normal is too small for the stage. Everything in life must be magnified to be effective on the stage, so when an actor steps into the performance space, they need to increase the magnitude of their existence.

2. Memorization: The actor's recall doesn't need to be perfect, but they need to demonstrate an obvious effort toward memorization, with some calls for lines, but not to the extent that the prompter must feed the actor each sentence. Memorization focuses primarily on two concerns: silence and struggle. Long periods of silence are an indication of memory lapse. Repeated pausing and heavy sighs are other signs. Anything that negatively impacts the flow of words should be eliminated from your performance. This does not mean actors must talk nonstop while performing. Actors pause when appropriate, espe-

cially if the pause is in the script, but it needs to be evident that it is the character pausing and not the actor going up on lines. Some problems actors can anticipate include getting words mixed up, mispronouncing words, saying the wrong thing then going back to correct it, and putting the wrong emphases on syllables. Actors can improve vocal performances by practicing their speeches out loud infinite times. If you can't do infinite times, still strive for infinity, at least temporarily. Saying the words aloud can create muscle memory in an actor's speech apparatus and this physical recall will instinctively aid actors in performance.

3. Characterization: The actor is making specific choices about the character rather than speaking and moving in generic fashion. Characterization means that the actor has fully invested in the identity of the character and is no longer being themselves. The actor moves, talks, stands, gestures, and emotes as the character and not as themselves. The primary concern this early in the class—and for this first monologue when you are being graded on a performance before you have even been taught practically anything about acting—is to not drop character. Keep character consistency, stay in character, all the way through, no matter what happens. Stay the character, do not revert to you, even if you must call for line or some other error occurs.

4. Vocal performance: Actors must be heard. No matter how fine the performance, if the audience does not hear it, it is the same as if it did not happen. The actor's job is to communicate the script to the audience, and for that to happen the actor must transmit the words to the receiver audience. While actors must utilize adequate volume levels, they do not want to be loud all the time. Another aspect of vocal performance is vocal variety, including seemingly natural changes in volume, pace, tone, and quality as when people speak in a normal setting. Some things are loud while others are quiet. Some things are fast while others are slower. Some things are high, like a soprano voice, or low, like a bass voice. Some things are smooth while others are rough. Try to make your performance sound like natural speech even though you are highly artificial. Pronunciation and articulation are also key to vocal performances. Actors can research word pronunciations through dictionary websites and apps, and word pronunciation websites and apps are also available. Plus, a student actor should not be afraid to ask. There is nothing wrong with asking a professor, a librarian, or anyone else how a word is pronounced, especially in school where everyone is present to learn. Another tool is YouTube, which contains many instructional videos focused on word pronunciation.

5. Physical performance: Focus on body language, gestures, and facial expressions. Body control is essential to success. On stage, every movement is a symbol of something going on inside the character, so actors should try to keep their bodies from telling audiences things that contradict the words the actors are saying. Beware of fidgeting, busy feet, and distracting body language or posture. Gestures need to be utilized, in moderation. One extreme is dead hands, the other is painting the air. Avoid dead hands and over-gesticulating. Your target zone is somewhere between stoned zombie and The Flash conducting an orchestra. Anything that supports or illustrates a message without distraction or the appearance of artificiality is desirable. The face is part of a physical performance and is a wonderful tool of communication. Actors should show how they feel about what they are saying with their facial expressions. The face is a screen upon which actors project the expression that illustrates how their character feels about the words. A rose gets one face; a pile of feces gets another. A loved one gets one face; an arch nemesis gets another. For Mister Fantastic, The Thing gets one face, Dr. Doom gets another. Do not over-exaggerate, but the face should be alive, fluid, and expressive. Make sure your hair is out of your face, and if you are wearing a hat, please remove it before you start your piece. Bad hair days are unfortunate, but I've had a bad hair life. Regardless, audiences need to have visual access to the actor's face and should not wear a hat unless the costume is designated as necessary by the script.

As a final request for effective performances, each monologue needs to begin with the actor's name and the source of their monologue, as in "Hi, I'm Rodney Whatley, and I'll be performing a piece from the play, *Doubt*."

With all of that in mind, who wants to go first?

Exercise 1

1. Do vocal and physical warm-ups.
2. Perform monologues.
3. All those not performing should take notes on performances and prepare to participate in feedback sessions. Please write notes down so that we don't lose any contributing material.

Homework

Next class: Perform Monologue #1 for a grade.

Acting I Monologue #1 Evaluation

Student _____ Grade earned _____

Energy
- Did actor appear enthusiastic about performance?
- Did actor have an appropriate level of energy?

Memorization
- Long periods of silence?
- Superfluous pauses?
- Did actor appear to struggle with words?

Quality of characterization
- Did the actor commit fully to the character?
- Did they stay in character?

Vocal performance
- Volume
- Vocal variety
- Pronunciation and articulation

Physical performance
- Body language
- Gestures
- Facial expressions

Lesson 4
Monologue #1 Performance Day

1. Perform vocal and physical warm-ups
2. The entire class should now take out note-taking tools, a writing instrument like a pen or pencil and paper, or electronic device. If you use an electronic device for notes, set it to silent.
   A. Set all devices to off or silent.
   B. Turn off vibration modes, as these make noise also.
3. Once someone has performed, the next performer does not begin until the professor has finished filling out the previous student's evaluation sheet.
4. All students will be participating in the Circle of Feedback once performances are done. Please take notes on each of your classmates' performances so that you can participate in the Circle of Feedback.
   A. Your goal is to identify two strengths and two weaknesses of each performance.
      a. Strive to look for two areas where the performer can do better so as to advise on how they can improve their acting for future assignments.
      b. Next is two strengths, or things the performer did well. These are like compliments, and who doesn't like compliments?
5. The professor will take notes and evaluate each performance today, then use that to formulate your grade after class. Grades will be reported during the next class, and the graded evaluation sheet will be yours to keep at that time.

Methodology for the Circle of Feedback

1. Circle up. The class will go around the circle and hear strengths first. Each student in turn will reveal only strength notes.
2. Once everyone has given strengths, the class will go around the circle again discussing weaknesses and tips for improvement.

3. Both positive and negative notes are intended to help all actors improve as artists.
4. Actors being discussed: begin to learn how audiences receive the messages you send with your acting. Compare your intent with the audience's perception.
    A. Actors cannot argue with audiences, therefore students in the Circle of Feedback should not debate their critics. Try not to think of the audience as wrong, try to think of them as hearing a different message than you intended.
    B. If there is a direct question, a brief response from the actor is okay, but mostly when given the opportunity to receive feedback, it is better to listen than respond.

Lesson 5
The Voice and the Face
It's All in Your Head

As you embark on your actor training, keep your eye on the target. What is the target? We can find that out together in our journey as artists, but whatever it is, your target is not to "get it right." Actors can sometimes tie themselves into unproductive knots by focusing on "getting it right." There is no "right" or "wrong," because art is a different field than something like math. There is art that works for some audience members and art that does not, but even if it only works for one in eight billion people, it is not wrong.

There is no perfection in acting. As Diane Keaton (2011) says, "What is perfection anyway? It's the death of creativity, that's what I think, while change, on the other hand, is the cornerstone of new ideas" (193). Embrace change, enjoy the journey, and always move forward. Besides, since humans are imperfect, can we even give a perfect performance? I posit that there is no such thing as a perfect performance, and that if one ever occurs, it will cause the universe to explode. Please do not achieve a perfect performance and therefore destroy all of existence.

Urinetown

People speak every day. This practice of oral communication, playing scenes in life with other people, is one reason why people without actor training decide that they want to be actors. This is partly where the urge for amateur and community theatre comes from, which is interesting because we can run and toss a ball back and forth, but the urge to play amateur and community football is much less universal, perhaps because of the greater chance of physical harm with football. This is not necessarily true, as acting can be very dangerous. I have suffered grievous injuries onstage and witnessed great harm befall others. I once saw an actor playing a *Dungeons & Dragons* knight screw up his fight choreography and get hacked in the face by a goblin queen. His face was split open and we had to call an ambulance. He ended up with a formidable facial scar that made him look like a bloodthirsty pirate, which is kind of cool, but still—no one wants to get hacked in the face.

Stage speaking has much in common with life speaking, but they are not the same. In real life, people need less breath support than actors speaking onstage; in real life people can speak merely from their head and throat. Voice placement is not as consequential for life as onstage; people can speak from the back of their throat, and other than irritating a crusty old person like me (by the way get off my lawn), all is still well, as long as the person being addressed by the back-of-throat speaker can hear them.

Speaking in life can be small. Speaking onstage must be large. I once directed an afternoon of one-act plays for a high school dual enrollment class, and one of the actors refused to project during rehearsals. They were concerned that the manner of speaking needed, stage speaking, was artificial and the actor wanted to make sure that their performance was, in their own estimation, authentic and real. The show opened and was a great success. Afterwards all the cast's friends rushed up and offered congratulations to all except that one actor who had refused to speak up. That actor came to me later and reported that everyone had uniformly told them that the actor had been inaudible, and the audience could not hear a single word that the actor had uttered. The actor said that they had learned that stage speaking was not the same as life speaking.

If you have had vocal training, like singing in chorus, you may have heard the phrase, "Sing from your diaphragm" (pronounced *die-ah-fram*). This means that you should sing using your abdominal muscles to push the air out of your lungs, up your vocal canal, and out of your mouth with strength and power. The same technique applies to stage speech: actors who speak from their diaphragm are using the set of muscles in their torso, the same muscles used when doing crunches or sit-ups.

Exercise 1: Breathing and Speaking

1. The class stands. Each student breathes in. Students' shoulders do not move, and chests do not expand. Students' guts extend outwards like an alien from the Sigourney Weaver classic science fiction movie, *Alien*, is going to pop out of their tummies. Then, like doing a sit-up, students engage those muscles to push the air out with control and power. This supplies their voices with great strength and resonance.

2. Throat tension causes damage and loss of voice. All students should relax their throats. Then, place one hand on your throat. Tense your throat so that you can sense what tension feels like. Students should then relax their throats so that you can sense what lack of tension feels like. Students speak from their diaphragms, improvising words, monitoring with their hands for throat tension level. Students continue to pay judicious attention to throat tension until they achieve a state where tension-free speaking is as natural as breathing.

Stage speech requires projection: volume and aiming the voice. In life, if there is a conversation between two people, it is simply those two people involved, but on stage there is another participant. On stage it is at least a three-way conversation between two scene partners and the audience. In life, a person aims their voice at the other person; on stage the actor's aim needs to include the audience.

In monologue circumstances, the actor is usually playing straight out to a spot on the back wall, their point of address. "Point of address" means to whom the character is speaking. Instead of standing in profile, as though talking to their point of address, the actor faces the audience as though it is the other character, or the other character is standing behind the audience.

If an actor aims their face up, or down, or backstage, that is where the sound will go. It is like their mouth is the business end of a Nerf Blaster. The sounds actors make are projectiles emerging from the Nerf Blaster: wherever the actor points their mouth is where the sound will go. It is vital that actors not exclude the audience when aiming their voice. Point your Nerf Blaster at whomever you wish to hear the sounds emitting from within.

For an Acting I class, an actor's vocal identity need not include extreme accents; a *Good Fellas* New Yorker, a *Forrest Gump* Alabamian, or a Shakespearean Londoner might best be left to subsequent acting classes, or dialect coaching. As actor training intensifies in difficulty and expands to take on more challenging characterizations, an actor's stage vocal identity will have the chance to evolve. For now, be your own best voice: loud, clear, and expressive.

Exercise 2: Vocal Identity

1. Individual class members take turns volunteering to stand up before the rest of the class. They each give a short speech. The rest of the class listens very closely to the speaker to identify speech characteristics.
2. Do we have accents? Do we need to do anything about them? What could we do?
3. The speakers attempt to improve their speaking abilities. Repeat the speech while attempting to strengthen identified weaknesses.
4. Experiment and try things. There is a chance that it will sound weird to you. I once had a teacher tell me that if I feel stupid or weird while doing an acting exercise, chances are I was doing it right.
5. Individually, each member of the class takes the performance space. Each member can do something that makes them sound weird, makes them self-conscious, that performed anywhere else would make them feel idiotic or ridiculous. Abandon all self-consciousness, ye who enter here.

Urinetown

Sounding stupid or weird can be frightening. Have courage. Alan Arkin (2011), a founding member of Second City, said of his time there, ". . . we were in an arena where we were allowed to experiment. To change. To grow. And not only that, we were allowed to fail. *Allowed to fail!*" He laments how civilization frowns on failure, "But how in the world are we to grow if we don't fail?" He concludes, "And if we don't grow, we decay. . . . Nothing in our universe is static. . . . At Second City we weren't allowed to decay" (44–45). All beginning actors can benefit by adopting his attitude.

In this class students are allowed to experiment, to fail, and to learn. Yes, at some point all students will have to perform their monologues or scenes for a grade, but the grade reflects whether or not the student has done the work, not how much talent they may be perceived as having. If the student does the work, if the student properly rehearses, these efforts will be obvious, and the student's grade will reflect the student's hard work. The only reason a student might have to worry about their grade in this class is if the student has not done the work. If the student does not do the work, it will also be obvious in the performance, and the grade will reflect that student's lack of effort.

You may say to yourself:

> YOU: Self?
>
> SELF: Yes?
>
> YOU: What about microphones?
>
> SELF: What about them?
>
> YOU: Why do I need to learn to project when professional actors on Broadway, touring shows, and regional theatre have body mics that pick up everything they say, amplify them so that every person in the last row of the house can hear all that they say and some things they only thought about saying?
>
> SELF: Why are you asking me? I'm you. If I know, you already know and there's no need for you to ask me. Also, why are we in Walmart at three a.m. wearing pajamas?

Actors are best served by not depending on electronic amplification. Theatres at the community, college, university, and professional level can opt to only mic actors when producing a musical so that actors can be heard above the full orchestra. (In my day I had to do musicals without body mics and project my voice over the orchestra unaided. I also had to be heard over the growls of the dinosaurs and saber-toothed tigers.) The purpose of the microphone is to amplify the sounds an actor creates by using proper vocal technique, not to replace volume and projection.

At this point I would like to share my frustration with the abbreviation for the word "microphone" being spelled "mic." When you use it in the past tense, as in, "They're miced up," it reads like the actor has been attacked by small rodents. I am tempted to replace the "c" with a "k" but without the "e" like in the name "Mike." But then "mik" could be just as confusing as "miced," especially if there are actors or characters named Mike in the show. I fail to fathom a solution to this grammatical quandary and every time I type "mic," the proofreading program on my computer tells me I have misspelled something again and underlines it in red. Infuriating is the kindest word I can think of to describe this situation.

Exercise 3: Fully Engaged Speaking

1. The actor must fully engage the entire speaking apparatus. All students stand and make sure that there is ample room around them so that they do not bump into other students or the furniture. Move desks and chairs against the wall to create a clear space as needed.
2. Students should make their posture erect. Follow these instructions: visualize that a steel wire projects from the top of your head and runs down the length of your spine. Something pulls on the wire, elongating and elevating your body. Make sure your shoulders are back and your head is not thrust too far forward.
3. Students should fully inflate and deflate their lungs. Expand lungs to full capacity and speak out all the air. Once lungs are empty, take your next breath. It matters not what thou dost spake, thou mayest improvise a speech or recite lines thou hast previously memorized. (Sorry, got pulled into the Renaissance for a moment. Back to business now.) Students should make sure they are not crunching up their torsos, which obstructs lung functions.
4. Students should relax their necks and free their throats of tension. Test throats for tension as you speak. Everyone speak for thirty seconds. In the words of John Cusack, *Say Anything*.
5. Students should use their abdomens. Follow these instructions: expand your abdomen when you breathe in, engage your muscles to push air up and out. Now do so while speaking. Fully utilize your mouth, no ventriloquism here. Move your lips and jaws when speaking. This is enunciation, which means properly and fully forming each syllable's sound, also known as "chewing the words." When an actor finishes a performance their face muscles should feel used.
6. Chewing words:
   A. Individually, each student should take a turn standing before the rest of the class and speak a speech, I pray you.
   B. Each student should improvise a speech or recite one that the student has previously memorized. Students should imagine that they are speaking to a robot on the phone and that they must clearly enunciate, or the robot will not be able to provide the students with desperately needed services.
   C. The rest of the class will observe each individual student's attempt at over-enunciation and provide constructive, helpful criticism.

Heck yes speaking in this manner is going to feel weird, which means that the student is probably doing it right. The real challenge is for the student to make the rest of their face appear normal while their mouth works overtime. This will improve with practice. The secret to success in the restaurant business is said to be "Location, location, location." In performing arts, the secret to success is "Practice, practice, practice." Practice need not make perfect, but it can lead to vast improvement.

Exercise 4: Vocal Exercises

I. Diaphragm work
   A. Stand erect, feet shoulder-width apart, toes pointed forward, shoulders back, head up.
   B. Breathe in deeply and completely, making sure shoulders remain still, your chest does not expand, only the gut protrudes forward.
   C. Exhale forcefully while making a steady "Ah" sound until the lungs are completely empty. Once they are empty, be silent.
   D. Repeat. Repeat. Repeat.
   E. Change sound to "Oh." Repeat. Repeat. Repeat.
   F. Turn to an actor next to you. Monitor each other's performance and offer correction as needed. Repeat steps C, D, and E.
II. Relaxed throat work
   A. Continue proper breathing, posture, body stance.
   B. Actors should place one hand around their own throat.
   C. The actors should perform "Ah," "Oh," and "Mmm" sounds while monitoring their throats for tension.
   D. Actors should choose a study buddy actor from among actors next to them.
      1. Each partner place one hand on the other actor's throat simultaneously.
      2. It can be unnerving to trust an acting partner to touch your throat. Trust falls!
         a. Volunteer needed to perform a trust fall with the teacher catching.
         b. Dare the teacher be the one falling back. Would anyone like to volunteer to catch the teacher?
         c. Those willing to participate may pair up and trust fall each other.
      3. Each partner monitors throats for tension as each partner simultaneously creates sounds. Each partner should offer correction as needed. Repeat Step C under these conditions.
III. Posture Work
   A. Establish good posture.
   B. Create a clear space in the middle of the classroom by pushing furniture to the side.

C. Each actor should walk about the space while maintaining perfect posture.

D. Divide class into two groups. Each group line up facing the other group, creating a tunnel between the two groups that stretches from one end of the classroom to the other. Each individual student take turns walking the length of this body hallway, striving to have perfect posture as the student walks. Once each student reaches the end of the tunnel, classmates need to critique the walk. Class should continue the exercise until all students have walked.

IV. Enunciation Work

A. Please follow the professor line by line in a performance of this soliloquy from *Hamlet*, exaggerating the movement of your jaw, lips, tongue, and other meaty accoutrements to create the sounds:

> *To be, or not to be: that is the question:*
> *Whether 'tis nobler in the mind to suffer*
> *The slings and arrows of outrageous fortune,*
> *Or to take arms against a sea of troubles,*
> *And by opposing end them? To die: to sleep;*
> *No more; and by a sleep to say we end*
> *The heartache and the thousand natural shocks*
> *That flesh is heir to, 'tis a consummation*
> *Devoutly to be wished.*

B. Please follow the professor line by line in this modern adaptation of the medieval morality play, *Everyman*, and this speech from the character GOD.

> *Everybody is dissing me. All they care about is what they can get, nobody thinking about me, my righteousness; they are all about carrots and forget that I do not spare the stick. I showed them how they should be, shed my blood, died for them and they forget that? I gave them everything. And they have left me in the cold. All seven sins, that's right, deadly sins, you want pride? They got it. Covet stuff? Oh yeah. Wrath? Everybody be trippin', dude. They believe lechery is a good thing now, if it gets them on TV or YouTube or something it's a good thing. Ain't no angels on YouTube! And it's getting worse every year. I'm going to have to have a group reckoning, because if this crap keeps up, people gonna be worse than animals. They gonna do cannibalism, they gonna eat up everything decent. They done straight up betrayed me, dude. You think anybody is asking for mercy these days? No, they think money solves everything. I got to do them right, put the fear of God into them. Literally. I'm gonna start with Death. Yo, Death, get out here my brother!*

32   Acting: Year One

Doubt

V. Solo Performance Work
   A. Actors should take turns stepping before the class. Actors should perform a short speech utilizing the concepts exemplified in the previous exercises, all at the same time. The speech can be a repeat of the actor's first monologue, some other piece that the actor has previously memorized, an improvisation, or anything. The actor needs to talk, giving the class a stage speech.
   B. Once everyone has performed this short speech, the classmates and the professor will assess and critique each performance, discussing them aloud. Notes should be taken so that critiques can easily be shared with classmates. All will perform first, then the class will go back and share critiques.

Exercise 5: The Face

1. The class, speaking in unison, should recite the alphabet, taking time with each individual letter to fully explore the sound.
2. Actors should magnify, exaggerate, and carefully observe the contortions their mouths must perform in order to create the sounds.

   The audience cannot read an actor's mind or tell what the actor is feeling. In order to communicate thought and emotion to the audience, the actor must perform physical actions that the audience can interpret. If a person feels anger, what is a physical action that person performs while feeling anger? The actor creates that action in the hopes that the audience who witnesses it will think, "Hey look, that dude is pissed, he punched that monkey." (No monkeys were harmed in the making of this paragraph.)

Physical actions include facial expressions, or facial gestures. Like a person's hands and arms, an actor's mouth, nose, eyes, and eyebrows are all appurtenances that the actor can move to communicate with the audience. When reciting palaver from memory, the face is often unresponsive, because the actor is focused on the task of remembering. While saying words one has memorized is an integral part of acting, acting is not a simple demonstration of recitation skills. The illusion of acting created by actors is that the character has not memorized lines. The actor's face must be involved at a greater level than when someone merely recites words.

A character's thoughts and feelings lead to speaking. The "illusion of the first time" is an acting term meaning that although the actor has said the lines numerous times, the character has never said them before. The character thinks, has an emotional reaction to that thought, and then as a result of the thought, speaks the line.

The main facial activity actors need to accomplish is to manifest how the character feels about what they are saying. To be clear, the process of think-feel-speak needs to be wholly created, each step completely done

Doubt

34   Acting: Year One

without a blurring of procedures. An actor cannot do Steps 1 and 2 only, or Step 1 and then Step 3, or Step 2 and then Step 3. It must be Step 1 (think) . . . Step 2 (feel) . . . Step 3 (speak). However, this does not mean that the actor performs a step and takes a pause, performs another step and pauses, and then performs the final step. Due to the incredible speed of thought, think-feel-speak may, and in most cases should, appear to happen simultaneously, even though the actor is performing each step separately, completely, and in order.

Exercise 6: Encoding Work

You have a large vocabulary. There are many ways to say something.

1. Let's imagine that I am looking out of my office window. I observe something. I say, "That red car is slowly moving west, while that airplane is flying quickly by, going south-southwest." What word could I have said instead of:

    A. Red

    B. Car

    C. Slowly

    D. Moving

    E. Airplane

    F. Quickly

2. In life, people subconsciously thumb through their vocabulary and pick the best word to express their exact thought, seemingly instantaneously. Once they pick the word, their connotative feelings, or how people feel about all they associate with that word, come into play. They show on their faces how they feel about the word they have chosen. At this point, students need to write down things that they associate with the following words. Students should try to come up with three things for each word. These things can be one other word, a phrase, a sentence, however the student needs to express the association.

milk	gas	dirt	mayonnaise	work	slob
jerk	rose	union	cheese	oyster	dog

3. The professor can now go around the room and poll each student to determine what everyone wrote down regarding each word. As the professor calls on students, those students will read aloud their reactions.

4. The professor should repeat the list from Step #2. The professor will say the word from the list, and then all students will repeat the word. This time, as students say each word, students should express with their faces how they feel about the word, the association and connotative feelings the students have for that word.

To create the illusion of the first time, actors must appear to recreate this process. Actors' faces are big tools for showing audiences their characters' thoughts and emotions. The actor's eyes and eyebrows are great mechanisms, as are their mouth and nose. The actor's nose can serve as a pointer, like an index finger on their face. The nose can serve as a device for focusing the audience's attention, in that they will look where the nose points.

In addition to illustrating thoughts, emotions, and the thinking process, the face is also a screen upon which can be projected emotional reactions that the character has to physical stimuli. People's five (perhaps more) senses are how people communicate with the physical world. An actor's face can tell the audience how the character feels about what the character sees, hears, smells, feels, and tastes. The face can also communicate feelings about ESP experiences. Most of these stimuli are imaginary for the actor. The actor must imagine what the stimulus is and react according to the character's needs when appropriate. In our next exercise, the class will react to imagined stimuli.

Exercise 7: Stimuli Reactions

I. Visual

   A. The class should create a list of things that characters might see. For instance:

   1. Beach sunset

   2. A Chihuahua running towards you.

   3. What are some others? Once the class has a list, they can move on to step B.

   B. The class should divide in half. To do so, form two lines, each line comprising a team. Each team should now face the other so that each team can monitor the other's performance. Team members should partner with the actor from the other team who stands across from them. Students should position themselves so that only a yard or so separates one team member from the member's exercise partner. In case of global pandemic, a separation of six feet is advised.

   C. Team One, react to the visual stimuli as the professor calls it out. Team Two, observe Team One.

   D. Now Team Two react to the visual stimuli as the professor calls it out, while Team One observes.

II. Aural

   A. Create a list of things characters can hear.

   B. Team One, react to the reading of the list while Team Two observes.

   C. Team Two, react to the reading of the list while Team One observes.

III. Olfactory
   A. Create list of smells.
   B. Team One react; Team Two observe.
   C. Team Two react; Team One observe.
IV. Sensation
   A. Create a list of sensations, or things people can sense, like dampness, heat, cold, pleasure, pain, and other sensations.
   B. Team One react; Team Two observe.
   C. Team Two react; Team One observe.
V. Taste
   A. Create a list of tastes—foods and drinks perhaps. Think of a favorite food. Think of a least favorite food.
   B. Team One react; Team Two observe.
   C. Team Two react; Team One observe.
VI. ESP
   A. What are some extrasensory or supernatural sensations a character might react to? Being blasted by Superman's heat vision? A Jedi Knight using the Force against someone? Defending against a spell cast by Lord Voldemort? Create a list.
   B. Team One react; Team Two observe.
   C. Team Two react; Team One observe.

This allows actors to make specific choices about their characters. Great acting comes from making specific choices, because those choices come from a world the actor creates for their character. The actor's reaction to that world makes the character fully formed, alive, and true to the audience. Having these goals, says Alan Arkin (2011), accomplishes several things:

> *First it makes it impossible to have stage fright or to be self-conscious. There isn't time. You have something to accomplish. Second, it allows you to be alive without self-judgment.... This emotional context will give you a felt connection to the character you are playing, so that when you go into the scene you won't be entering with an intellectual idea but with the sense of the character. (146–47)*

Going through this process keeps actors so busy and so active and so alive that audiences will be stunned by the energy, vibrancy, and living quality that the actors bring to the stage.

Arkin (2011) also says that art is "the direct injection of the actor's experiences into the audience, and that this transfusion is the highest purpose of all the arts" (9). Actors then need to draw from themselves, go onto the stage, and create true life.

Lesson 6
Cold-Reading Audition
Iceberg, Right Ahead!

If you were on board the *Titanic*, those words would be bone-chillingly frightening. Equally frightening to an actor can be the announcement that the audition will consist of cold readings from the script. Both can be imminently disastrous. While climate change is taking care of some of the dangers of icebergs, this chapter is meant to reduce the fear instilled in actors by the appearance of the white printed page on the horizon.

A cold reading is when an actor is handed the script and called upon to mount the stage with acting partners and begin reading with zero preparation. If the actor is given a chance to look over the script, be it for ten minutes or ten days, it becomes a warm reading. There you are at the audition, minding your own business when the director calls your name, gives you a script and a page number, assigns you a character, identifies the starting line of dialogue, and then cheerfully announces, "Okay, let's hear it."

You may ask yourself, "Self, why do we do cold-reading auditions?" And your Self may respond, "I can tell you why the industry of theatre uses cold readings as a practice, but if you are asking why we personally do it, meaning you, I would have to say it is because we are masochists." Directors use cold readings because they could be the closest thing to an actual talent meter in that cold-reading performances offer a glimpse of how much raw talent the actor possesses.

It is also a way of being inclusive, especially in educational and community theatre. At college and university, new theatre majors or students from other majors may feel sheepish at the prospect of a memorized monologue audition. A reading audition can serve to ease these students into play participation, thereby increasing the quality of their lives by immersing them in the magic of play production. Likewise, in community theatre volunteer actors may have little experience or training in acting, and should a memorized monologue be demanded of them, they might instead simply decide not to get involved. A community theatre without volunteers is an empty shell, and so the community theatre encourages participation from inexperienced actors however possible.

Why would a professional theatre organization do it? It's that whole "talent meter" concept. Consider all that is required for a successful cold-reading audition: first, a cold-reading audition requires that an actor think fast. There is no faking that. With little or no knowledge about the script or the character, actors must use their critical thinking skills to make snap judgments about important issues of dramatic theory:

- Who is the character?
- What is the character doing?
- What does the character want?
- How does the character feel about the other characters?
- Is there subtext in the lines?

With scant evidence, the actor decides and acts upon those decisions moment to moment in real time. This can tell a director the actor's relative level of intelligence, theatre knowledge, knowledge of acting principles, critical thinking skills, and level of mind-body coordination. Mind-body coordination for the actor means how quickly the actor's body can do what the actor's mind thinks.

The cold-reading audition also demonstrates the actor's level of confidence in their acting abilities. The actor should be bold and instinctual, making decisions and acting on them. Actors in a cold-reading audition can't hamper themselves with worry as to whether their choices are good or bad; right or wrong, they make choices and execute them. This trust in instincts can be an indicator of whether the actor will succumb to stage fright and how they will hold up if something goes wrong in a performance. An actor who makes a choice and trusts it is less likely to break character during a performance should something go awry. And something will; it always does.

There are two ways to prepare for a cold-reading audition. The first one transforms the cold read into a warm read but is only possible if it is a published play and a copy is available for purchase from a bookstore or online retailer, or available for loan from the local library. If so, then you can get a copy of the play ahead of time, do some research, and practice reading aloud to yourself dialogue from the script. It is best to read the whole play aloud because auditioning actors cannot know what part a director might ask them to read.

The director may cast gender-, race-, and age-blind, considering all actors viable for every part, a style of theatre called "Inclusionism." Or the director may simply need an actor to read opposite another actor, and so may ask the auditioning actor to read a character for whom they might not be considered in an audition run by a conventional production. Some directors make decisions during auditions that are unknowable to humanity. The secret to success is giving the director what they want, even if to the auditioning actor what they want makes no sense whatsoever.

Actors must trust their instincts. Dame Judi Dench (2010) tells a story about Sir John Gielgud's propensity for changing his performance due to his over-reliance on the opinions of others. "There is a story," she says, "that may be apocryphal that somebody said to him in a play, 'I don't think you should wear the brown shoes, I think that the black shoes are better.' Somebody else said, 'I think the brown shoes are better,' so he wore one brown and one black shoe" (28). Trying to please everyone is a waste of time, so actors should focus on pleasing themselves with every performance. Actors should trust their choices, commit to them, and play them fully.

The second way to prepare for a cold-reading audition is to read aloud from any material, not just the script for which actors are auditioning. Actors read aloud standing, full-voiced, with proper posture and full commitment. They can be seated at their desks in their offices if need be, and they can do it with other people around, although actors need to be prepared to receive verbal and physical deterrents should they do so, like shouted profanity, thrown shoes or garbage, or—at the minimum—venomous eye rolls. However, the best thing for actors to do is to find a space where they can be alone, take a book, script, whatever, open it up, and have a go. Auditioning actors should read aloud as often as they can, because the best way to get good at it is to do it repeatedly and frequently.

The elements of success at cold-reading auditions include proper vocal technique, facial expressions, script grasping, blocking, playing focus, body language, and gesturing. The emphasis in the cold-reading audition is the voice and the face, so actors must diligently create their moments. Special attention should be paid to voice technique in order to exaggerate it even further. The cold read is like acting for radio drama, or voice acting for animated television, film, or web projects. Actors should over-enunciate, retain fluidity, and readdress expressiveness, taking it all up to a higher level.

The same is true for facial expressions. While the voice seems to be the major component, the face is equally important. Actors should intensify their responsiveness and creativity, not to the point of mugging, but magnified. The face is the prominent visual focus that the director will fixate on as the actor reads.

This is partly because when you are reading from a script, your hand gesturing ability is cut in half. Holding the script in only one hand leaves the other hand free to gesture, which effectively halves the actor's gesturing capacity. Audiences are like T. rexes: motion attracts their attention, and since the actor has only one hand now that the other is anchored to the script, more attention will be focused on the actor's face. Do not try to compensate for this by increasing the gesture activity of your free hand. Use it at about the same level you would in any performance, to support and illustrate the words without distracting from them.

Regarding holding the script: auditioning actors should not hold the script up close to their faces. This hides the face from the director. An actor may be tempted to focus so much on the words, perhaps from a fear of losing their place on the page, that they lose track of their face and deny the director this key auditioning component. Not occluding the face can be tricky. To determine the proper placement of the script, hold the script in your hand with your arm straight down, then raise your hand all the way to your face by bending your elbow. Lower your hand halfway between these two points. Now raise it just a bit more, maybe an inch or less. Stop! This is the optimum script position for reading, as it allows for maximum unobstructed view of your shoulders and face when reading. This works if you are auditioning in a room, and the actor and director are standing or sitting on the same level.

It is a little more problematic when the stage is a raised platform and the director is seated in the house several feet below the actor, as in most auditoriums. This situation the actor must play by ear, but the good news is that the hallowed dictum of theatre sightlines, "If you can see them, they can see you," still applies. Follow these instructions: periodically make sure, while reading, that you have a clear view of the director's face. Try to be unobtrusive about it; do not stare. You do not want the director to think you are playing the scene to them; most directors prefer the actors pretend the director is not there.

Auditioning actors should play out, as though the point of address is floating in front of them. Do not play stage right or stage left, as though interacting with the character beside you. This may seem overly presentational, but in this case you would have a script in your hand anyway, so how realistic can you be? If you spend too much time in profile, talking to your audition partners, you are hiding half of your face. At least cheat out and keep your face one-quarter open, halfway between profile and straight out, and alternate that regularly with brief profile shots and longer periods with your focus fully downstage, or fully out. It is a fine line between ignoring your scene partners and limited sharing with them. Actors should not ignore their reading partners with their physical orientation, but their focus needs to be out towards the audience so that the director can see what goods thou dost offer.

One way in which auditioning actors should ignore their partners in a cold reading, though, is when it comes to blocking. Do not perform the blocking indicated in the script's stage directions. There are many reasons for this:

1. The reading actor could lose their place in the script, causing awkward pauses in the reading as they try in vain to find it while repeatedly apologizing for losing it. Directors can find these dropped character delays frustrating.

2. You may make your scene partners uncomfortable. Initiating uninvited physical contact with a stranger, even at auditions for plays, is a bad idea.
3. If you try to do the blocking, your reading partners may stop and ask, "What are you doing?" That would be bad.
4. The director may have already blocked the scene and might find your version distracting. Instead of watching and evaluating your audition, they are comparing your blocking to theirs. What if they think you got it wrong? Or worse, what if they think yours is better than theirs and then resents you for it? Just kidding. People are wonderful. That would never happen.

Blocking is something that comes during the rehearsal process; most directors do not expect a reading actor to create blocking. Attempting to perform blocking during a cold-reading audition will weaken the reading actor's performance, so avoid it. Freezing in place is not required. Uncomplicated movement, when inspired by the text, is good in that it can show the director that the actor has a good sense of space and a strong command of stage movement skills.

Body language is extremely important. Auditioning actors need to demonstrate that they have optimum control of their physical instruments. Observe good posture, eliminate unnecessary and distracting movement, and make of your body an expressive tool. Avoid adjusting your clothes and repeatedly touching your hair. Be aware of and control your feet. Getting a case of happy feet, where your feet or legs are in constant, unfocused, anxiety-induced movement can be theatrically fatal.

Another thing to avoid is trying to figure out what the director is thinking by how they act during the audition. You may ask yourself, "Self, how come they only called me to read once? Does this mean they hate me and never want to hear my voice again?" No. Maybe? It could mean the director loved the actor so much that they do not need to hear that actor again. It could mean they are a confident director who only needs to hear actors once in order to make casting decisions. Or it could mean the director is in a hurry to get home to Netflix and chill. Maybe *Better Call Saul* or *The Witcher*.

"What if the director calls me to read several times, as in like a whole bunch of times? That means I'm totally cast, right?" Nope. If this happens to you, it could mean that the director simply does not realize how many times they called you. Maybe they are a conventional director and there is a shortage of your gender identity at the audition, and the director needs someone, anyone, to read with what they perceive as the opposite gender. Or maybe it means nothing. Actors should not read into it. In a cold-reading audition, the only things actors should read are the scripts. And the cast list once it is posted, but that goes without saying, so why am I typing this?

Finally, while it can be a daunting situation, actors cannot let nerves get the best of them in a cold-reading audition. Failing that, the actor should at least never admit that they have cold feet. The other actors might try to read them. It's because of the word "cold." See what I did there? Cold reading? Cold feet? Hello? Is this thing on?

Cold Reading Exercise

1. The class should perform vocal and physical warm-ups
2. When called, students should report to the performance area and read from the scripts provided as indicated by the professor.
3. As for the rest of class, when not in the performance arena doing readings, they take notes on the quality of each actor's performance and be prepared to discuss the strengths and weaknesses.

Acting I Cold Reading Performance Evaluation

Student Name _____ Grade _____

Vocal Technique
1   2   3   4   5   6   7   8   9   10

Facial Expressions
1   2   3   4   5   6   7   8   9   10

Script Grip
1   2   3   4   5   6   7   8   9   10

Stage Presence and Movement
1   2   3   4   5   6   7   8   9   10

Body Language
1   2   3   4   5   6   7   8   9   10

Gestures
1   2   3   4   5   6   7   8   9   10

Playing Focus and Eye Contact
1   2   3   4   5   6   7   8   9   10

Line Interpretation
1   2   3   4   5   6   7   8   9   10

General Notes:

Lesson 7
Script Analysis
And How Does That Make You Feel?

Script analysis is an abyss that can go as deep as the reader wants. Because of its form and function, the script is only a collection of clues provided by the playwright. The actor must take these clues and deduce the truth of the character only hinted at by the script. This chapter is specifically about selecting monologues to be memorized and the preparatory work actors need to do to get them performance ready. Scenes will be discussed in a later section of the book. An Acting I class is like a beginning diving class: one does not start by jumping down the Marianas Trench. There are limits as to how deep one goes in the beginning; as training and experience progresses, actors can choose to go deeper if they wish. To maximize the script analysis experience, it is imperative that actors select good dramatic material.

Script analysis is vitally important. Actors need script analysis because acting is storytelling. Actor Judi Dench (2010), who has periodically served as a director, describes some of the advice she gives to actors she has cast. "What I did say to the cast, probably every day, was, 'I want you go out and tell the story. You must never forget that there is a story here to be told, and that's what our business is'. . . . I'm interested in somebody coming out and re-creating this story as if it were for the first time" (118). One cannot tell the story, as Dame Judi advises, unless one knows what story to tell. The words are only part of the story.

When picking a monologue this semester, and later a scene, students should choose material from plays that have been published and are considered part of the dramatic literature canon. Doing so helps prepare actors for their future training and their professional career by exposing them to works they might be cast in as a working actor. Competent theatre students or theatre professionals are expected to be familiar with these plays. They are regularly revived in theatres around the world, so knowing them prepares student actors for future auditions. The main job of a theatre actor is to act in plays, so early training like an Acting I class needs to focus on material from plays that have been successful on the stage.

Imagine being in a green room and suffering humiliation as everyone else in the green room laughs at an actor when they say something like, "*Oedipus?* What's that? I like to pet cats, not eat them," or "*Hamlet?* No thanks, I'm really hungry; I'll have the full-sized ham sandwich." They might even be asking, "What's a green room?" A green room is an area for actors to wait prior to going backstage to begin the show. No matter what color that room may be, it is called the green room.

In this class, once an actor has selected a monologue, the actor should—and I can hear the groans from actors who competed in drama festivals in high school and have heard this directive a million times, so say it with me now—"Read the entire script." Ain't theatre fun? This may sound like a big ask, but it really is not. The average play takes less than two hours to perform, and since most play scripts consist of only dialogue with very little stage directions, they don't take much more than two hours to read.

Alan Arkin (2011) laments actors who only read their lines or scenes of a script. He says:

> *In a well-written piece every part has a function, every character is necessary to the whole. Sometimes the function of the character is obvious, sometimes it has to be searched for, sometimes it just adds to the tone and mood. An actor's exploration becomes much easier if he examines the material from the viewpoint of discovering his function in the piece. (143)*

Knowledge of the whole script is the actor's first resource when it comes to being savvy about what a character is saying, especially if there is any exposition in the monologue referencing previous events in the play. Without this knowledge, the actor cannot know what is important to the character and what is not, which can lead to poor acting choices.

Recently I was helping a student actor prepare for entrance auditions and scholarship auditions at a major university. We were thumbing through some plays I had recently purchased, looking for speeches that had appeal. I came across an amusing speech about eating Mexican food in a movie theater in a play called *The Flick* by Annie Baker. It was a collection of words and it was funny, so I suggested the speech to the student. Later I read the entire script and the speech took on much greater significance when placed in context. Avoid taking things out of context. Do not be like the politician or celebrity who responds when a controversial quote is aired by saying, "That was taken out of context!" You do not want to be the one taking the quote—or in this case the monologue—out of context; own the entire experience so you know where everything fits.

This is also a way of showing respect to the script. As a young actor, I never met a script I could not change. I always thought I knew better than the playwright how to say something. Yes, there are bad scripts out there, but I realize now that most of the time when I changed things, I was wrong. The work of the writer deserves respect. Judi Dench (2010) says, "Noel Coward was always a stickler for having his lines spoken exactly as he had written them, and I think he was absolutely right, you should respect the author's creativity" (223).

Even if you think the script has problems, you should honor it. Sidney Poitier, discussing the ending of the film, *The Defiant Ones,* observed that some people did not like how it ended. He said he disagreed with the character's actions, "But as a professional actor my job was to create the character with the sensibility to conduct himself in the way

Sherlock Holmes and the Adventure of the Suicide Club

he behaved in the end, and that's exactly how I played him." Poitier said the movie's point of view is determined by the director, who made a good decision, as did Poitier by playing the writer's vision. "And indeed on my part for playing the character as it was written" (Poitier 2000, 104–105). If an actor does not like what the writer has provided, the actor should choose a different script. As Stan Dean, a late director friend of mine used to say, "When you're the writer, we'll say your words. Until then, stick to the script, if you don't mind."

When preparing to direct *Laughter on the 23rd Floor,* I discovered that Neil Simon's contracts specify that directors and actors cannot change his words, not even the dirty ones. David Mamet's dialogue, often written complete with nonverbal sputtering, is written for the rhythm of the sounds and needs to be performed intact. And paraphrasing Shakespeare? Just do not. Even an audience who does not know Shakespeare can tell when actors veer off-script. Kenneth Branagh tells a lovely story about improvising dialogue during a production of *Henry V* in his book, *Beginning.* He realized he'd misplaced an integral prop, and so he incorporated instructions in how to retrieve the prop to his fellow actors into his performance. He could tell that the audience immediately knew that something was terribly wrong because the nature of the dialogue was so changed.

I was once in a production of Shakespeare's *Richard II.* A fellow actor forgot his lines. He informed the king through his improvised dialogue, "I know not what to say, my liege. I don't, I can't, I know not, I don't know

Sherlock Holmes and the Adventure of the Suicide Club

what to say." The actor playing the king turned to look at me. I shook my head and shrugged my shoulders, signifying, "Hey, you're the king, you fix it." By this time the audience had started giggling.

Actors can show respect to the words by doing extensive pre-performance work. This is called preparation, and students need to prepare. I believe that 90 percent of acting is the actor alone in their room working with the script. The actor then brings the fruits of that labor to share with their coworkers and audience. The actor's preparation must be extensive. Perspiration leads to inspiration, and preparation provides perspiration. Shawn Levy, author of many actor biographies, writes of the rigorous pre-production preparation that is a hallmark of Robert De Niro's work. De Niro is easily one of the greatest actors from the 1970s through today. Levy (2014) writes, "He could drive directors and acting colleagues crazy with his obsessive focus on detail, but he learned to build a character from the outside in, to allow the inner life of the men he played to emerge through a firmly established air of external realism" (10). Once actors know the details of the character, they can focus on creating the inner reality that drives their performance.

Levy (2014) goes on to say of De Niro, "He became famous for doggedly researching his roles and rehearsing until he had internalized a character, until he had, in his phrase, 'earned the right to play a person,' after which he would disappear into that person's skin entirely" (140). That is a great work habit. One way to be great at something is to identify someone who is already great in that field, find out what their process is, and adopt their process as your own while you create and develop it. Mr. De Niro and his work habits are worthy of emulation.

Analysis means going beyond the script. In some instances, actors make far greater contributions in creativity than playwrights. Writers give the bare bones of the character, perhaps a physical description and the words that the character says. The physical description may be moot, for once the actor is cast, the character essentially looks like the actor. If a director casts a person of color as Superman, a woman as God, or a short, thin person as Lenny in *Of Mice and Men,* all apologies to Jerry Siegel, Joe Shuster, Larry Gelbart, and John Steinbeck, but in those instances, that is what those characters now look like. The primary contribution of the playwright is providing the words that the characters say. The actor must fancifully create the rest of the character based on the scant clues provided by the playwright. As Judi Dench (2010) says, "Sometimes I do have a lot of difficulty learning the lines, but the real difficulty is working out why the character says the line, and what is going on between the lines, which is often more important than the line itself" (96).

In addition to being an expert on the script, the actor is required to be an expert on human psychology. The character is a fictionalized person drawn from the nonfiction psyche of the playwright; while the character is not real, the playwright is. To understand character behavior, the actor must be able to analyze the behavior of humans like the writer. Shawn Levy quotes boxer Jake LaMotta discussing Robert De Niro's analytics when the actor researched LaMotta for *Raging Bull:* "De Niro was, LaMotta told a reporter as far back as 1977, 'more qualified to be a psychiatrist than a psychiatrist. He goes very deep. He's telling me things about me that I never knew'" (Levy 2014, 231). The actor becomes an expert on human psychology because figuring out why people do things in life is an invaluable tool for figuring out why characters do things in plays. Even nonhuman characters are actually slivers of the playwright's personality in writing.

For a beginning actor in an Acting I class, the main research and preparation for a character in a monologue or scene derives from an analysis of the given circumstances of the play. The given circumstances are:

1. Who
2. What
3. When
4. Where
5. Why
6. Way

Just like a journalist! So, if you have parents or friends and family who tell you, "You've got to have a back-up plan for when you fail as an actor," tell them you are also training for a career as a reporter or psychiatrist. Actor training provides a stable base for both. Also, actor training is good for potential trial attorneys, so tell kin and kind that you don't just have a back-up plan, you have a Plan A, Plan B, and Plan C. It's perfect!

The first element of given circumstances is to know who the character is. This includes basic information about the character like the character's name. This is true even if the playwright does not give a full name, or any name for the character. If no name is given, or only a partial name, the actor must fill in the blanks. People have names, so if the character is a person, they need a name. If in the script the actor's character is called "Person in Elevator," the actor must give the character a full name.

Nonhuman characters are based on some aspect of human nature and the human experience. All characters share a common root in that they are born from the writer's imagination. If an actor is playing a supernatural character, they also need backstories, albeit supernatural ones. Just like in Marvel Comics, all superheroes have an origin story. When Wolverine first appeared, nobody knew where he came from, and nobody much cared until he came to be very popular under the writings of Chris Claremont on the rebooted *X-Men* comics starting with issue #94 in 1975. Over a period of decades, writers and editors pieced together Wolverine's backstory until they had one that seemed to satisfy their audience. Actors must do the same work as a team of Marvel writers and editors for their character even when the character is supernatural, obscure, or otherwise incomplete. This applies to all other character identity traits as well as their backstory.

Other data you should consider among the given circumstances is the character's gender identity. Most works prior to the mid-twentieth century only offer the gender options of male or female. In this age of sometimes gender-blind casting, this can be negotiable, but at this stage of analysis, the actor is simply trying to figure out what the playwright intended. An actor playing a character is not an endorsement of that character's behavior traits.

The specific age of the character is next. The actor is not simply a teenager or someone in their twenties, no more than as of this writing I am a person in my fifties. In the year 2022, I am fifty-eight; that is a specific number. Therefore, a character, even if the script identifies her as "a woman in her thirties," needs a specific number for their age. The actor can even give their character a birthday if they like. That is recommended, because then the actor has something more to play off of, and it can tell the actor what astrological sign their character was born under.

The character's marital status and relationship history should also be considered. Single characters are different from married characters, and divorced characters are different from both. I have been in all three stages, and I can testify that a person's relationship status has a genuine impact on how they view almost everything about their life. Some secondary questions might be: Is the character lonely being single, a happily married spouse, or a happily divorced survivor?

Educational level is next. While intelligence level and educational level are not always causally related, great intelligence is perceived to be coupled with extensive education. Are there idiots among people with advanced degrees? Oh yes. There are also intelligent people who are almost wholly uneducated. By "educated" I mean someone went to school, including college. I have found, though, that most intelligent yet uneducated people were not uneducated, rather they were self-educated. Multiple Pulitzer Prize winner August Wilson quit high school at the age of fifteen because he was falsely accused of plagiarism. According to Britannica's website, "He turned to self-education, reading intensively in a public library and returning to the Hill District to learn from residents there." Actors must ask, how smart is the character? What is the character's educational level? Actors can play characters smarter than themselves by saying the lines convincingly. Ask anyone who has ever played a doctor, and they'll say you just memorize the lingo and speak with confidence, like Leonardo DiCaprio in *Catch Me if You Can*. It is more challenging for an actor to play someone who is perceived to be of lower intelligence. Actors can help their approach to playing the character by determining whether or not their character is smarter than they are. Ah, that age old question: who's smarter, the actor or the character?

Finally, for Acting I, the identification of the character includes an examination of the character's economic and social status. Rich people are different from poor people. Why are rich people so different? Because they can afford to be (*insert rimshot here*). While it is true that money cannot buy happiness, it can certainly rent it for a while. Having a lot of money does not solve all your problems, but it does solve all your money problems, and since money makes the world go around, having riches changes the focus of a character's existence. In a capitalistic world, or any world where currency is a necessary tool for existence, money ensures survival and affects the quality of life for the character. Being miserable in a penthouse is different from being miserable in the gutter. Just ask Jean Valjean from *Les Misérables*.

The next given circumstance element is *what*, as in "What is the character doing?" Characters are pursuing an objective or goal, something they want. Going all the way back to the ancient Greeks with Aristotle's descriptions of plot, up to and beyond Stanislavski's observations about superobjectives, a major tenet of acting is that characters in plays want something, and the plot is a record of the character's journey, the pursuit of that superobjective. Students in this class play characters that want something; that is why the characters speak. The dialogue delivered by students in this class are actions taken by their characters in pursuit of a goal. Acting students assess what their characters want and the actions they are performing in order to get it.

To clarify terminology, it should be made clear that "objective" has many synonyms, such as intention, purpose, target, and goal, to name a few. Different acting techniques developed by performance theorists, professors, or directors may use these terms interchangeably and thereby cause some confusion. From my experience, I have developed a system that clarifies the terminology, and to which I will refer in this text. The system is illustrated by the following word picture:

A play can be divided into acts; acts can be divided into scenes; scenes or monologues can be divided into a beat, which is considered the smallest unit of dramatic action. A beat can be as simple as this: imagine a scene in which the characters are eating dinner. Your character, Grandchild, wants the mashed potatoes, and so speaks to Grandma, who is between the Grandchild and the mashed potatoes.

>GRANDCHILD
>Grandma, can you pass the potatoes?
>
>GRANDMA
>Oh baby, it's so cold in here.
>
>GRANDCHILD
>Yes, and those hot potatoes will warm me up.
>
>GRANDMA
>What's your name, baby?
>
>GRANDCHILD
>I don't know, the writer didn't give me one, but I need those potatoes, I'm so hungry. I'm Grandchild, okay?
>
>GRANDMA
>Oh baby, I can't hear you, what?
>
>GRANDCHILD
>Grandma, I'll love you forever if you give me those potatoes.
>
>GRANDMA
>Oh baby, you so fat and they have so many carbs, you don't need no potatoes.
>
>GRANDCHILD
>GIVE ME THE POTATOES OR I'LL POP A CAP IN YOUR ASS!
>
>GRANDMA
>Okay, baby, here you go.

Your character now has the potatoes, and the beat is complete. Then your character turns to another character, Sister, and says, "Sis, can you pass me the gravy?" This begins a new beat. The goal of the scene is to eat a meal. Breaking the scene down into beats is like breaking up the running of a mile into each step.

Each beat has an aim. That aim leads inexorably or in a straight line to the accomplishment of the scene's goal. The goal leads inexorably to the accomplishment of the act's objective. Each act's objective leads inexorably to the accomplishment of the play's superobjective. Creation of this path makes a straight shot, or throughline, that the character takes in the play, with no side journeys or distractions. It is a determined pursuit of what the character wants and provides motivation for every action the character takes in the play.

Please note that the divisional term "aim" has the fewest letters of the four terms, with only three letters. The next larger one, "goal," has four letters, leading to the second largest term, "objective," and finishing with the largest word, "superobjective." The size of the character's desire is reflected by the size of the word chosen to represent it, so the terminology is designed to help navigate the plot. If the actor is talking about the largest word, the actor is talking about the play. If the actor is talking about the smallest word, then the actor is referencing the beat.

Next in given circumstances is *when*, as in when the action of the play takes place. Chronologically speaking, the actor needs to know the year in which the character lives. In order to make the most informed character choices conceivable, the actor needs to be as specific as possible. For example, people are different at 4:00 a.m. than they are at 4:00 p.m. People can be one way in the morning, depending on whether or not they are a morning person, another way at lunch, another way in the afternoon, perhaps drowsy and in need of a nap, or maybe they only truly come alive once the sun goes down. People can also be seasonally affected and therefore different in the summer than they are in the winter.

The actor needs to decide when the monologue or scene takes place. Perhaps the playwright provides this information in the stage directions or makes references in the dialogue. If not, then this is a decision left entirely to the actor. What year is it? What season is it? What month is it? What week within the month is it? Which day of the week is it? Which hour of the day? As people, we exist at a finite point in time and space. To create the richest portrayal, characters need to do so as well.

Speaking of space, the next given circumstance is *where*, moving analysis elements from chronology to geography in order to determine where the scene or monologue takes place. Again, hopefully the playwright will at least have given the actor a clue as to where the character is, but it is important to note that the set of the play is not the same as the geographical location of the character in the character's world. The set is the responsibility and thus the product of the scene designer, usually designed in collaboration with the director and other technical artists. The director contributes during the conception phase, or the thumbnail sketch period, and other technical artists may be consulted as the designs progress. For the monologues and scenes of this class, students serve as their own directors, so students should apply their own imagination to the dialogue and stage directions to interpret geographical clues.

Sherlock Holmes and the Adventure of the Suicide Club

The geographical location refers to the world of the character. What continent, for instance? If it is North America, then which country? If the United States of America, which state? Is it in a city or a rural setting? Which city, town, or principality? Is it indoors or outdoors? Is it a commercial building or a private residence? If a private residence, is it an apartment or a house? If it is in a house, which room? What is the layout of that room? Where is the furniture? Where are the doors and windows? Where is your character in that space?

The actor needs to create a complete place that the character exists in and is affected by the same way that actors exist in and are affected by their environment in their reality. Fully imagining the character's surroundings will create an environment to which the actor can respond. This complete creation of environment will help when it comes time to block monologues or scenes. Blocking is how the actor and director plans their physical actions, when and where they move as they speak the text. If there are concrete environmental parameters, blocking must take them into account and interact with those elements.

Lesson 7—Script Analysis   53

If the scene takes place on Earth, the actor's imagination has less work to do than if the scene is set in an alien environment. The actor's workload increases with alien worlds, but that alien encompassment still needs to be intimately created. Characters do not exist in a vacuum, unless, of course, the play is set in a vacuum. I have never read a play set in a vacuum and really, I do not think I ever would. Not to judge a play by its setting, but how interesting can a play be when set in a void? "The time? Never. The place? Nowhere. Join our hero as they struggle to find a point of reference."

Why tends to be a tricky given circumstance ingredient. *Why* is what motivates the character's pursuit of the goal. For example, why does the Grandchild character from our earlier scene want to eat dinner? Food is necessary to survival and a source of strength. In a well-written script there will be clues, either subtle or blatant, as to the character's motivation. Heck, in some scripts the playwright just comes right out and says it, but this is not always the case. It is also not always the case that actors are working with good scripts. Regardless of the script's quality, the obviousness or lack thereof to the motivation's presence in the script, it is the actor's responsibility to come up with the character's motivation. It is the actor who is in the coziest relationship with the character. It is up to the actor to decide why the character does what they do.

It is fine if the reason why is not in the script, or extremely well hidden. The motivation of the character is not the writer's job; it is the actor's. Let's imagine that we are playing the Tin Man in *The Wizard of Oz*. We are holding our axe at the time the script calls for us to go into the song, "Jitterbug." The Tin Man is afraid, feeling threatened by the minions of the evil Witch. But the choreographer has designed a dance that requires the Tin Man to put the axe down. Why would the Tin Man put the axe down? The simple truth is that we need to put the axe down so that we can perform the choreography. It is our job as the actor to come up with a reason for why our character would put the axe down. The actor's motivation is to perform the choreography, the axe is preventing the Tin Man from doing that, so the Tin Man needs to put it down. For the character, perhaps the actor decides that the Tin Man wants to defend against attack but does not want to inflict the grievous injuries on a living being that the axe would create, and so puts it down. Whether it be the verbal action of saying the lines or the physical action of the blocking and choreography, the actor creates the character's motivation.

The final given circumstance element necessary for script analysis in a beginning acting class is *way*, as in what method or what way will the character use to achieve the goal? These methods can fall into one of two categories: positive actions or negative actions. The character can use honey to catch flies, or vinegar. The character can be nice or mean. There is an episode of *Cheers* in which Frasier opines, "You can catch more flies with honey than with vinegar," and Woody replies, "That may be true Dr. Crane, but actually you catch the most with dead squirrels." In this class, actors will not have a dead squirrel option, only mean, nice, or some combination of the two.

As the world of drama can be roughly divided into two broad hemispheres, comedy and tragedy, so too can the methodology of the character's actions be hewn into being either mean or nice. You can threaten someone, or you can cajole them. You can slap someone, or you can pet them. You can yell, or you can purr. There is a vast range between the two, and actors can explore the entirety of both terrains. There may be a combination of the two, or an alternating pattern that goes back and forth between them. The way the character behaves while pursuing their goal is the *how* of given circumstances. You can be mean, you can be nice, but you cannot be a dead squirrel.

This chapter has detailed the minimum script analysis that actors need to do for every performance piece they attempt, especially in this class for this semester. This level of script analysis is a good starting point and will provide a solid base for students in this class to build upon for the rest of their training.

Homework

1. Students need to select a play. My advice is to go to the school library, a treasure trove of academic resources. Search the electronic index for plays. Ask a librarian for help if need be. That is what librarians are for. Ask them, they like it.
2. Students can ask their professor for access to scripts. Professors often have a large library of plays they are happy to loan out.
3. Students can also consult online and digital resources. You know what? Libraries have access to data, too. Libraries are good.
4. Students should select a script. It needs to be a script the student can read in its entirety.
5. Students should pick a character from a play to which the student feels a strong connection.
6. The student picks a monologue for Monologue #2. Assignment guidelines instruct that this be a serious monologue from a play written for the stage and published. Time limit is not to exceed fifty-nine seconds and no shorter than thirty-five seconds. Sixty seconds is too long.
7. Students should perform an analysis of their monologues using the technique described in this chapter. Students should write their analysis work down and be prepared to discuss their analyses in class.

What Is a Serious Monologue?

Most published plays come with a genre description. The two hemispheres of drama in this case are tragedy (or serious plays) and comedies. There are many types of serious plays, the purest form of which is tragedy. There is also melodrama, heroic drama, romantic drama, domestic drama, modern tragedy, and tragicomedy, among others. All of these are acceptable serious plays from which to draw monologues.

This may sound like a lot of hard work, but here is the student actor's list of duties:

1. Pick a script
2. Pick a monologue
3. Analyze the monologue
4. Memorize the monologue

And, yes, it is hard work. If acting were easy, everybody would be doing it. Yet even though it is hard work, it can also be fun. Sissy Spacek, when working with Jack Lemmon, was amazed at how Lemmon "could turn his acting on and off at will. . . . I on the other hand, would stew all day long if I had an emotional scene coming up. If the scene was at five o'clock in the afternoon, I would start winding myself up hours before, getting ready, and by the time the scene finally rolled around, often I would already be spent." Lemmon advised her to trust herself more. "Go easy on yourself," he said to her. She said, "He was an inspiration to me, and living proof that all great acting doesn't have to involve suffering" (Spacek 2012, 25–206).

So work hard, but have fun. It starts by picking good material, so get to it.

Lesson 8
The Body
I Like to Move It, Move It

As countless as the stars in the sky are acting teachers and their systems, or methods, or techniques, or whatever jazzy names we give for the processes they recommend in order to produce good acting. If I add to that, the results might be *The Rodney Routine*, *The Whatley Way,* or the best (worst?) of all, *What Acting?* Probably better not to clutter the intellectual terrain.

My concept of good acting, in relation to teaching Acting I, is that good acting comes from utilizing three areas in conjunction. When organized exertion occurs from these three areas, the student actor's unification of effort is more likely to produce artistically relevant acting work. Those three areas are the body, the mind, and the soul. Full engagement in each is required for good acting, and each has a separate role to play. This chapter focuses on the body. Robert DeNiro once observed of technique, including proper use of the actor's body, that "Technique is concrete. . . . Acting isn't really respected enough as an art. Your body is an instrument, and you have to learn how to play an instrument. It's like knowing how to play the piano" (Levy 2014, 264). If audiences knew how much thought, work, and effort went into stage movement, as opposed to real-world movement, respect for actors would grow and intensify.

The first rule regarding the body, and the reason for the song reference in the chapter title, is that actors have to move it, move it. See what I did there? Movement is a performance requirement for the lessons in this class. An actor weakens an audition monologue performance if they only stand in place and talk.

Audiences do not come merely to hear a play; they also come to see it. The actor's job is to communicate the play to the audience through time and space, and practically every production involves movement on the part of the actor. I once attended an audition workshop where students from a variety of schools took turns performing contrasting monologues. Some students would begin their first monologue all the way downstage center, turned slightly to stage left, or one-quarter open. For the second monologue, they turned one-quarter open to stage right. That slight change of focus was their only stage movement. I found it incredibly limiting and visually uninteresting. It also failed to let me know if any of those actors could capably move about the stage space, and if they were auditioning for me, that would have been problematic.

An audition is where actors display their capabilities to a potential employer; actors need to show off all their performing arts wares, not just their ability to speak from memory while standing still, which might work if the actor is auditioning for *Stonehenge: The Musical*, otherwise not so much. The monologue is a performance; just like a scene or a play, it requires blocking. When blocking a monologue, however, actors need to realize it is different from the performance of a full play. The actor's playing goals are different, so the actor's playing technique needs to be customized and adapted.

Big

The monologue performance is a condensed and intensified version of regular play acting. It is busier and more magnified than regular acting. The basic concept for movement is that actors want to show casting directors that they can move and what they look like from various angles. Actors want the casting personnel to see their right profile, their left profile, and their face's full-frontal view. In this, the movement design ensures that the actor's face is delineated from at least three different angles. Therefore, auditioning actors could incorporate a motivated stage left cross and a motivated stage right cross somewhere in their blocking to accomplish multi-angle viewing as naturally as possible.

These crosses also show that the actor has a command of stage movement technique. Actors need to show that they can carry their torsos erect, that their legs move confidently, with power, that they control their body and have eliminated all purposeless and distracting movement. Casting personnel need to see that the actors are a physical presence of some magnitude on the stage that demands audience attention.

By the way, actors do not have to limit themselves to just those three sides. If you are in an audition situation, you can turn your back to the audience as well. As an actor I have had directors yell at me, "Never turn your back to the audience!" But if the material calls for it and the actor feels it is intrinsic to the moment, the actor can turn their back to the audience, if it is a motivated movement and not just for show. The movement needs to flow logically from the action of the speech. There is vocality to consider, too, as the actor must not sacrifice audibility. If the actor's back is turned because they are facing upstage, they must speak louder and enunciate more than when facing downstage. And when the actor turns their face back towards the audience, they must return to their regular vocal volume level.

In this class, each of your student monologue performances will need to incorporate blocking and stage movement. The scenes that students perform later in the semester will also require blocking, but scene blocking is different from monologue blocking and will be covered in the twenty-first chapter on "Working with Others."

The main aspect of stage movement that differentiates it from real-world movement is that stage movement always has a purpose. There is no wasted movement. Everything means something. This is what gives stage movement its intensified, condensed nature, even more so in a memorized monologue audition. It is like a short story versus a novel: in the novel the writer can stretch out, sprawl, explore things; in a short story everything is there for a reason and handled with maximum efficiency, lest the story grow in length and then is no longer a short story, but a long story.

There must be a purpose to the actor's walk. Actors cannot just cross stage left at some point in their monologue because the exercise requires it. The character must have a reason for making the cross. Maybe the air conditioner is blowing on the spot they stand on, so they move to seek warmer climes. Maybe the light is better over there. Maybe they flee a threat, maybe there's a bad smell in the spot they now occupy, and they want to escape the odor. The actor imagines a reason, and lets that reason cause the character to cross from one spot to the next. The audience may never know the reason, but the actor does. The audience needs to see that the character has a reason; they do not need to know what the reason is. Most audiences will fill in the blanks from their own imagination, making them part of the creative process, which makes them treasure the work more.

To show that the cross has purpose, actors can pick a spot that represents the destination on the floor. Actors target the spot where they will stop the cross; in film industry terminology, this is known as their mark. The mark is the actor's destination. The actor looks at it. The actor decides to make the cross. The actor strides with purpose to the mark while looking in the direction that they are walking. The actor should not face out front while walking sideways, walk backwards, or sidle. Once the actor hits the mark, they can face forward and plant their feet. This style of stage movement implies that the character has somewhere to go, that the new place is where they are meant to be, and that they are there for a reason.

The actor's stance and body language bespeak purpose. Characters are in a state of perpetual need and are never at ease. When the character stands still, they are poised for action, ready to go in whatever direction is needed to avoid a threat or chase a prize. They plant themselves as someone who owns that spot of earth upon which they stand. Actors need to project a force field of authority, of energy, an orb of presence around themselves, like Violet in *The Incredibles* and the Invisible Woman in *The Fantastic Four*. It may sound esoteric and weird, but acting is sometimes weird. If actors visualize their force fields, people will feel it and take notice. And if the actor feels foolish while doing this, then they are probably doing it right.

Purpose in body language involves the elimination of unnecessary, random movement. In life, it may be okay to twiddle one's fingers, slap one's hands against one's thighs, shuffle feet or drum toes, but onstage all of those movements mean something to the audience. An actor twiddling their fingers could mean that the character is carrying a gun and is about to draw it and pull the trigger. Slapping their thighs could be a sign that their character is demanding someone come to them immediately, or that squirrels have invaded their clothes. An actor shuffling their feet could mean that they are nervous and drumming their toes could mean that they have to urinate exquisitely! Unless the actor intends to send these messages, these movements need to be eliminated from the actor's instrument.

Every movement, every pose, is equivalent to holding up a sign to the audience, because everything means something. In this way, stage movement, even in a non-musical production, is like interpretive dance: all movements are symbols and the audience will take every symbol as a message relevant to the performance's meaning. The actor's body must say what the actor means, otherwise the actor garbles the play's message.

And like sign language, the biggest physical communicating apparatus is that set of hands and arms attached to the torso. So, what do actors do with their hands? Mindy Kaling (2015) once observed this conundrum when discussing being photographed: "The most valuable thing I learned from Kim Kardashian is that your arm must never lie flat against your body. . . . I remember hearing her say that when you put your hand on your hip, it makes your arm look thinner and draws attention to your waist. I tried it and I loved it! So I started doing it whenever I was getting my picture taken" (20–21). Okay, so that quote is not really relevant, but it does point out how meaningful everything you do with your arms and hands is.

Big

Actors make sure their energy and awareness extends all the way down to the tips of their fingers. If an actor fails at this in performance, it looks like their arms are numb past their elbows. Avoid dead hands. This can be done by keeping the muscles in wrists, hands, and fingers slightly tensed as if ready for action. The actor is poised for possibilities and fully energized.

Actors' gestures need to support the words of the script and aid in conveying meaning. The best way to figure out what gestures to make is by watching people in real life. A great way for an actor to develop physical traits is by watching what people do and then imitating their movements. Over the rehearsal period, these imitated movements are refined and adapted to the character and the situation. The actor observes, imitates, and then enacts. Start with an imitation of someone, and then evolve that imitation into the creation of the character.

I once had a director who said, "Okay, let's run the scene, and if you feel like moving, then move, let's see what happens." We were all new actors afraid of doing something wrong. None of us felt anything except fear, so none of us moved. With gestures, no matter how awkward they may feel, the moves must be created. The actor must start somewhere. One place to start can be to use forced, big, and awkward gestures. Remember, if the actor feels foolish at first, they are probably doing it right. Actors must force themselves to perform arm movements and hand gestures, even if they do not feel a natural urge to do so. Make the gestures big. Over time and rehearsals, actors can reduce movements in size and adjust them to the words. Repetition will aid in the process of naturalization. With enough work, by the moment performance time rolls around, the actor will have a set of gestures that feel and appear natural, appropriate, and meaningful.

The next part of the body that actors spotlight is their visual focus. When performing a monologue, the actor is alone on the stage, but usually the character is not. For the actor, the character is always talking to someone else. Whoever the character is speaking to is where the actor's visual focus needs to be. The visual focus needs to be a point straight out over the audience so that for most of the speech the actor is giving the audience their full face. The visual focus is where the actor looks while speaking. Where the actor looks depends on what kind of monologue they are performing, what kind of address the playwright has given the speech. The most common kinds of address are other characters, a higher power, and the direct audience.

No characters, even classic Shakespearean characters in soliloquy, are ever just talking to themselves. A convention of theatrical acting is that whenever a character speaks, it is an action the character is taking in order to pursue an objective. The character wants something and so they speak. No character can achieve the objective by themselves, if so, there would be no play. The character needs others in order to achieve the objective that creates the need for speech—the act of communicating with others.

No line of dialogue is merely a line of dialogue; it is an action taken by the character upon another in order to achieve the objective. That other is either another character, a higher power, or the audience. In the case of direct audience address, the violation of realism's fourth wall makes of the audience a character in the drama and obliges the audience to directly participate in the scene.

When the actor's point of address is another character, actors should avoid playing the monologue as though they are enacting the play, pretending another actor is onstage with them, invisibly playing the role. This is a weak choice because it makes the auditioning actor, the character who is visible onstage, perform almost the entire scene in profile, turned to the side and away from the audience. The auditioning actor needs to imagine that the director is sitting in the center of the audience. The actor's face is a flashlight lens. The actor should shine their beam on the director, but if the actor plays to the side, they are shining their beam several feet to the side, missing their target. The auditioning actor needs to imagine that the other character is out front, suspended over the audience, at the actor's eye level. The common advice is to play to a spot on the back wall, and in most theater spaces this is good advice. But do not to stare at the spot the whole time. That would be like unbroken eye contact in a conversation, which can be a little creepy. Also, actors need to break eye contact when they perform a cross, as they need to look where they are walking.

If an auditioning actor breaks eye contact with the imaginary character in front of them, and then it's time to return their gaze to their imaginary partner, they must return their gaze to the same spot. This keeps visual focus from becoming fuzzy. The director needs to see the actor seeing what the character sees; it needs to be real and consistent for the actor. This can be hard because the actor is playing two roles simultaneously: their character and the imagined character to whom they speak. The actor plays their line, then imagines the other character's reaction to the line. The director needs to see the actor see the reaction and then how the actor reacts to that reaction. From the other character's imagined reaction, which the actor created, the actor has to create their own reaction and play it, and then they have to imagine the other character's reaction to their reaction again, and this chain of events continues until the actor gets to the end of the piece. It is like playing a game of chess with yourself in which you play both sides of the board.

The second type of address is to an unseen presence; not another character in the play but still within the reality of the play's world that does not acknowledge the presence of the audience. It may be God, it may be a force of nature. Heck, the character may not know who they are talking to and may believe they are talking to themselves, but the actor knows they are not talking to themselves, they are addressing a nonhuman external force. Part of the reason writers like Shakespeare used soliloquies was so that they could write long, beautiful poems for the audience whose motivation to come to the theatre was in part to hear that beautiful use of language. Another reason for a soliloquy was so that the playwright could share the character's inner thoughts with the audience.

Those motivations are fine for the writer, but they do not work for the actor. It is like when there is exposition in a script. Imagine an opening scene between a butler and a maid, and in their conversation the audience finds out all they need to know about the main characters and the situation in order to understand the play. The writer's motivation may be to get that needed expository information to the audience, but the actors playing that scene must properly motivate their characters with objectives. The characters' objectives cannot be to provide information to the audience because to them the audience does not exist.

The character in a Shakespearean play performing a soliloquy, or a character in a more modern play with a monologue, or long, uninterrupted speech when they are alone onstage, is not talking to themselves, they are talking to a higher power. This especially fits when considering the three major forms of dramatic conflict: person versus person, person versus self, and person versus nature. Nature includes things like gods, or nonhuman spiritual beings. Giant asteroids, floods, tornadoes, and dogs named Cujo also fall into that category.

The usual visual focus I advocate for beginning actors when emulating a speech that addresses a higher power is the same for when addressing another character, only higher. The actor should look out over the audience to that spot on the back of the wall, centered over the heads of the audience with a slightly elevated point of focus. The actor looking up signifies to people that the higher power under address is perceived by the character to be somewhere up above, like in heaven, for instance. An occasional elevated visual reference will help convey the message that the character is, in some form or other, praying or beseeching a higher power for aid in their desperate time of need, or looking for some deity to share in their celebration.

The third type of visual focus is direct audience address, in which the character is aware that there is an audience present and directly engages with them. This can be true of Greek plays as well as other classical plays. In ancient Greece and the English Renaissance, actors did not believe in the concept of the fourth wall and often interacted directly with the audience. This is true of some modern plays as well, especially ones that utilize a narrator character. Sometimes numerous characters share the narrator trait, as in John Guare's *Six Degrees of Separation*, which is written like the characters and the audience are chatting at a dinner party while the characters share recent events in their lives, like stories over drinks.

When performing a monologue of direct audience address, actors are making the audience the other character to whom they play. The actors should not just pick one audience member and talk to that one person, nor try to include everyone, which causes the actors' eyes and heads to be too busy with near constant motion. Actors need to find some medium ground that is between staring like a fixated stalker and someone who's overdosed on morning coffee. Actors can pick a few faces, at random, and engage with those audience members in order to guide them through the experience. In the absence of actual people in the audience, actors can use the empty chairs, imagining that there are people sitting in them.

Actors should not use the auditor, director, casting director, or anyone judging their audition—in the case of this class, the professor—as their acting partner; instead, use other members of the audience, real or imagined. The director is too busy evaluating the actor's performance to engage with the actor and may find the actor's efforts off-putting and distracting. For the director, it is like someone taking a test and asking after each question, "Did I get it right?"

In the case of auditioning for a play, or performing for a grade in class, it is too much like the actor is checking on the director to see if they like what they are seeing as the actor performs. It is like at the end of every sentence the actor is asking, "How do you like me so far?" In the case of the professor in class, it is like the student is asking, after each sentence, "What is my grade now? What is my grade now? What is my grade now?" Actors can strive to pretend that the judge is invisible or not even there at all, which also helps reduce stage fright.

Big

Another thing actors need to be wary of is how the audience members that they do engage with are going to react. There is no predicting what an audience member will do. Being reflexive and able to adapt a performance to the actual energy being received is great, but actors cannot let audience members distract them. If an audience member acts like a jerk, actors need to be prepared to stay in character and move on to someone else.

The next part of actor physicality involves using the actor's body, through blocking and stage business, to illustrate the actions of the words. Stage business is the small body movements the actor makes from moment to moment in the character's existence. In life, people are like great white sharks: they move constantly, or they drown. People, often even while asleep, are in almost constant motion, even when appearing to stand still. Stage directions and directors may give the actor the bigger motions, like blocking, but the smaller physical realities, or stage business, are usually the purview of the actor.

A strategy for figuring out the physical actions or body language that the character can portray to illustrate the action of the speech begins with identifying the action verbs in the speech. Take this speech from my play, *The Vinyl Id,* in which the character Avon is describing a traumatic event to another unseen character.

> *I was making a long drive for a job interview, about 800 miles one way. I left the afternoon before to drive all night, sleep the next morning, go to the interview in the afternoon. Around three in the morning, this is Friday night you understand, this truck **barrels up** behind me. Lights on bright, **weaving**, and he tries to **pass** me on the right, the breakdown lane. He gets about halfway around, then changes his mind and **slows down**, then he tries to **pass** me on the other side. He gets past me, then he thinks he's at his exit I guess because he goes to exit. Only there's no ramp there. And he figures this out about ten feet off the interstate. So he **swerves** back out. He's driving a big old Chevy truck, early '80s I think, otherwise he would never made it. He gets back on the road, by this time I know he's gonna **wreck** so I slow down just then we come to an overpass. He **hits** the guard rail on the left with his passenger side headlight. The truck **flips up** and around, the door **pops** open, he wasn't wearing a seat belt, out he goes. (Pause) He was wearing a ball cap, I saw it **float** off his head on butterfly wings. (Pause.) The truck **bounced** off the other guard rail, then went into a hundred foot **slide**, 113 I think the trooper said. The guy **slid** almost as far as the truck. I **slammed** on the brakes and pulled over. I **ran** up to him, glass **crunching** under my feet. When I got there he was still **breathing**. His tee shirt was pulled up over his big belly, beer gut. It was up over his face, I couldn't see anything but his eyes. They were open, he was looking at nothing. His stomach **lurched** with a **spasmodic** breath every few seconds. It was not normal breathing. There was a crown of blood **spreading** out, I remember he was wearing calf-high lace-up moccasins, and his head was **split** right up the middle, starting at his nose, like someone had **pounded** the letter V in from the top of his head. I could see his brains. Could see he was **dying**. By that time someone else had come, and they were **waving** oncoming traffic down because the guy was **lying** across both lanes. I pulled the shirt off his face to help him breathe, he stopped anyway. His necklace ran into his mouth, the pendant was **lodged** in his throat. It might have been a cross. I watched him **die**. I held his hand and I watched him die. I looked on his finger. He had a wedding band, so he had a family. For their sake, I **said a prayer** over him. I told the trooper, he said he'd tell the family what I did.*

The bolded action verbs are dynamic: *barrels up, weaving, swerves, wrecks, pops open, bounced, slammed, crunching, lurched,* and *pounded.* These and the others can serve as physical cues for blocking, body language, and gestures as well as facial expressions and vocal changes in quality. These action verbs serve as what I call spurs.

A spur is a word in the script that goads, impels, or urges the character to an illustrative and relevant physical action. These shifts in thought or emotion, a desire to be close or move away, a sign of vulnerability or increased defensiveness, are opportunities for the actor to create physical actions that are natural, seemingly spontaneous, and free.

When saying "barrels up," the actor could inflate and emphasize their chest and cross downstage. When saying "weaving" and "swerves," illustrating hand gestures or head-bobs might work. "Bounced, slammed, crunching, lurched" and "pounded" are all hard, violent verbs that offer powerful illustrative possibilities for the body instrument. The actor always looks for action verbs and explores the physical possibilities associated with those words to create a dynamic presentation of the body.

The final thing about acting with the body that I will point out is simply that it is just that: acting with the body. Actors physically perform the actions; it is not enough to think things or feel things. The audience cannot read actors' minds or sense the color of their aura, so actors must create an external manifestation of their inner existence.

Robert DeNiro, discussing his actor training, said, "There was a teacher who taught at Sarah Lawrence . . . and he said 'Just go on instinct.' And it kind of frees you because you get distracted with 'What's my character? What's my motivation?'. . . You forget in life people don't behave that way. They just do what they're doing; there's no thought behind it" (Levy 2014, 60). Actors want to achieve the appearance of that lack of thought and self-examination, and they can accomplish that through body acting. If the question is to do or not to do, the answer is *do it*.

Actors perform actions that symbolize the underlying emotion that caused that physical action. Based on what the character says and does, the actor identifies the emotion they believe the character is feeling. What physical action does the actor associate with that emotion? The actor may say, "If I am angry, do I pound my fist into my hand, or thump my chest? Do I make violent motions with my hand, or act like I have someone's throat in my hands and choke them out? If I am hungry, do I stroke my mouth or rub my belly?" Actors can explore a variety of physical actions and refine them through the rehearsal process.

Observation of real people is once more an actor's best research tool. The opportunity to go to a crowded park, mall, or food court, have a seat, and watch people is an incredibly valuable resource for actors. An actor sitting in a crowded public space can observe a wide swath of humanity experiencing a cornucopia of emotions and watch what physical actions people perform when they are in those situations. The actor can observe, imitate, and enact what they see.

Sissy Spacek (2012) relates the value of this process when she describes the research she did for her Oscar-winning performance as Loretta Lynn in *Coal Miner's Daughter*. She wrote, "I started following Loretta around like a puppy, trying to capture her body language and her accent" (185). Later she said, "I met her while she was playing some shows in Lake Tahoe and spent an afternoon tape-recording her while she told stories" (185). And finally, she noted, ". . . I videoed myself sitting in a chair with my tape recorder in my lap, playing and replaying Loretta telling stories. I would play that recorder and repeat those lines over and over until I kind of got my own version of her" (186). She did not win the Oscar for doing an impersonation. She took her observations of Lynn, started with imitating her actions, and evolved into her own portrayal of the character: a fictionalization of Loretta Lynn created to serve the needs of the script. Spacek's creation had a sense of truth to it, as it was rooted in careful observation of human behavior, and so Spacek was awarded with film acting's highest honor.

I won an acting award as a junior in high school participating in the one-act competition of the Alabama Trumbauer Theatre Festival. My character was a basketball player and described in the script as some kind of super-jock. In high school, I was a comic book nerd enrolled in chorus and drama who hung out at the local roller disco skating rink, so the world of high school athletics was far removed from me. I identified a multisport athlete who, in my estimation, epitomized the high school athlete. His name was Stan Spears. I followed him around campus, studied how he walked, moved, stood, gestured, held his shoulders, head, everything about his physicality. I started out imitating him, and through rehearsals evolved the performance until it fit the needs of the play. I received the "Best Actor in a Supporting Role" award that year. One of the best compliments I got from a judge was that, from the moment I entered, my character "exuded an air of athleticism about him." I naturally had to resist the urge to sniff my armpits, helped by a nudge from the elbow of my drama teacher, Mr. Dayton Long. When he heard "an air," he read my mind and anticipated my sniffing and stilled me before I could move. The judges thought my performance was incredibly natural. I was very proud in that moment.

You, too, can be an award-winning actor, just like me and Sissy Spacek. Just act with your body. And mind. And soul. The next chapter is on the mind.

Exercise 1

1. Students should identify key action verbs in their monologue.
2. Students should create blocking for their serious monologue.
3. Students need to design gestures to go with their speech.
4. Students need to determine their visual focus.
5. Students should determine gestures and movements appropriate to illustrate those action verbs.

Exercise 2

1. The class needs a few volunteers who are willing to take turns attempting to physicalize their speeches while the rest of the class watches.

Exercise 3

1. The class should divide into teams of three students each.
2. The teams should take turns working on their physical performance. While one team member performs, the other two team members watch, then the group confers on the performance as to how it can be improved.

Suggested Homework

1. An actor goes to a shopping mall that has the reputation and potential of being crowded. The student picks a day and time when the maximum amount of people will be at the shopping mall.
2. A student does people-watching for at least one hour.
3. A student records their observations in a journal of some sort and saves them for future use.

Lesson 9
The Mind—Changing Yours

To some, the body is nothing more than an animated piece of matter used to carry around the mind. Of the three areas an actor uses in order to be successful, the mind can arguably be considered the most important. The mind is that part of the actor that houses the intellect. Everything the body does is fueled by the mind. It is the place from which most of what the actor does originates.

Emotions are something more spiritual, and I will cover emotions, spirituality, and the soul in the next chapter. Just about everything else comes from the mind, which is why it is such a terrible thing to waste.

The most common reaction I get from audience members, especially strangers, when I meet them after a performance, is probably the same most other actors also hear from family and friends: "How do you remember all of those words?" That ability, which some call "memorization," comes from the mind. The mind is what makes an actor capable of preparing to play a role by doing things like research. Discipline, a necessary component of good acting, stems from the mind. Imagination, belief, and the ability to make choices are all products of an actor's mental abilities. Critical thinking is an especially important tool in life, but even more so for the actor who also uses it in the imaginary life they create for the character.

Before I left for college, my mom said, "Don't let classes interfere with your education." What she meant was that not all learning occurs in the classroom. One thing my undergraduate days taught me is that I lack the ability to teach myself Algebra. I really should have gone to that class more often. Another thing it taught me is that learning is a personal responsibility. I have had good teachers and bad ones, and students can learn from bad teachers as well as good ones, but most of my learning involved me and the campus library.

The same thing is true for beginning actors. It is not the professor's job or the director's job to train beginners or make beginners good actors. That responsibility lies with the student actor, just like it is an actor's job when cast in a role to research the part. In the case of audition monologues, by choosing a monologue, the actor has cast themselves in that role, and the responsibility of researching that role is the same as if Disney just cast the actor and is paying them $10,000,000 to do the job. For those of you equally bad at math as I, that is ten million dollars.

Great acting comes from extensive preparation. Sure, if an actor is born with great talent and natural ability, they might be able to give a great performance occasionally, but actors cannot depend on talent. Actors need to do the work, the preparation. Talent without craft is like lightning: no one ever knows when and where it is going to strike. Lightning is unpredictable and unreliable. Craft is like electricity: the actor turns on the light switch and the bulb glows until the actor turns it off. It is predictable and dependable. Depending solely on talent is not a path to greatness.

Levy describes how, in his youth, Robert DeNiro studied under Stella Adler:

> The Young DeNiro entered this emotional and artistic minefield possessed of a personal bent towards silence, observation, and nose-to-the-grindstone work that happened to mesh with Adler's ideas. If watching his mother and father at work had taught him anything, it was the value of application, self-scrutiny, doggedness. Art could, at least in part, result from elbow grease. (Levy 2014, 51)

DeNiro bent towards silence in class because when a person listens to themselves speak, they learn nothing new. Observation is integral because actors learn about acting by watching other actors and people. Application means applying oneself, doing tasks. Self-scrutiny is an honest assessment of the actor's weaknesses and it is the strength to recognize and address them. Doggedness means an unwillingness to give up, no matter how hard the work is or how frustrating it may become. Actors work hard.

Preparation is a herculean exertion. Sometimes it seems to lack reward, as the reward does not come until actors get to the performance, which may be weeks or months away. Actors must be good at accepting delayed gratification for their efforts. Alec Baldwin (2017) described Angela Bassett's work as Lady Macbeth on a 1998 Public Theatre production of *Macbeth* in which they worked together. "Angela was intense, kind and intelligent. But above all, she was prepared and this was instructive. She reminded me that acting was work. It's unique work, it can be enjoyable. But it requires an effort and precision that can't be faked or bypassed with good looks and charm" (251).

When researching a part, there is plenty of hard work for the actor's mind to embark on. The major source of information for enacting the character is the script from which it emanates. Actors should pay attention over the course of the play to what the character says about itself, although actors must be careful with self-descriptions. For example, a good person usually does not walk into a room and declare, "I am a good person," because that person's actions define that person as such and part of being a good person is being modest. Of greater importance than what the character says about itself is what the character does. Because of drama's condensed nature, characters in plays are defined by their actions even more than people in life. Finally, actors should pay attention to what other characters say about the character. Usually, these observations are more accurate than character self-descriptions because the other characters are more objective, although such is not the case if the other character has an agenda that puts it into conflict with the character the actor is playing.

Student actors can look for reviews of previous productions of the play, or other types of articles and books written about the script or productions of the script. Reviews of productions can be found in newspaper and magazine archives as well as educational and theatrical journals. In addition to reviews of productions, there may be articles or books that do a dramaturgical or critical theory analysis of the script itself and the characters within. Most of these resources should be available online.

In addition to looking for reviews, articles, and books on the play, students can look for critical or biographical writings about the playwright and other works that the writer has created. If the writer is alive, students can reach out to the playwright. When I was working on my MFA at Lindenwood University, researching the part of Ferris Layman in Jim Leonard Jr.'s *The Diviners,* I found out that Leonard was going to be at nearby Webster University to work on another of his plays. I reached out to the school,

Present Laughter

asking if I could interview Leonard for my master's thesis. He got back to me, and while he did not have time for a formal interview, we had a lovely phone conversation. You never know unless you try, so students could seek out contact information for the playwright and reach out. But no stalking. Always, no stalking.

The same is true for other actors who have played the part. In looking for reviews, students may come across the names of other actors who have assayed the role. Actors love to talk about their acting and why their take on a character is the right one. And in the twenty-first century, everyone is on Twitter, Facebook, Instagram, or what-have you, so students may be able to contact those actors and be like, "Hey, what's up with this character, yo?" The worst they can do is say no or block you, right? Well, if you take it too far, they can have you arrested for cyber-stalking. Do not stalk or harass people, okay? That's bad.

Another possible resource is YouTube. Students can access many videos online posted by people who have produced most plays, even though their productions legally specified that there was to be no recording of any kind, and if recorded, there was definitely not to be any posting of the video on the internet. Despite this copyright violation, all those videos are there, allowing students to look up recordings of other actors performing their characters. The main danger for the student actor is the temptation to imitate the other actor's performance. And of course, supporting copyright violators, which is bad.

Imitating another actor's performance is the same as copying answers from the person sitting next to you during a written test. It is an act of acting plagiarism. An actor is a creative artist, not a copy of a creative artist. If the actor imitates the work of another artist, the actor is not an artist, but a copier of other artists, tracing over the other actor's work and not creating the actor's own works of art. Be an artist, not an imitator of artists.

The final factor to be aware of when watching recordings of actors onstage is this: they all suck. I have been in a play, and somebody recorded it, and then I watched it, only to be horrified at how terrible the show was and particularly how horrible I was in it. I began to believe that everyone lied when they said it was great because it obviously sucked! If this has happened to you, you can relax; the performance was probably fine. The play performance is designed for the live audience sitting in the theater at the time of performance, not for the camera on a tripod at the back of the house. Because the play performance is so designed, the impact that any video of it has will be negligible when compared to the live experience. Still, one never knows when one will find something useful, so it never hurts to check on YouTube. Some scholars even post lectures and discussions of plays and characters these days instead of or in conjunction with writing articles and books, so student actors can also look for those.

Lesson 9—The Mind—Changing Yours   73

Discipline is another important aspect of acting that comes from the mind. Sidney Poitier (2000) wrote, "Upon realizing that I could be a better than utilitarian actor, I realized that I had the responsibility not as a black man, but as an artist, to exercise tremendous discipline. I knew the public would take my measure, and that was constantly in my calculations" (107). All actors have this responsibility. What does discipline mean? It means saying no to some things while saying yes to others.

Discipline means saying no to poor diet and exercise. In ancient Greece, actors trained like Olympic athletes, and while that may no longer be considered necessary, a healthy diet means actors are choosing wisely. Acting is a strenuous physical and even more strenuous mental activity. Actors need to properly feed their engines for the engines to run well. Exercise is also a good idea. It keeps the mind sharp and the body ready.

Discipline means saying yes to getting enough rest. No matter what, there are only twenty-four hours in any given day. What an actor cannot accomplish in one day can be put away until tomorrow. While there are implacable deadlines in theatre, like opening night for a show or performance day in class, failure to be ready by go time can usually be attributed to poor time management skills. Actors' deadlines are usually weeks from when they are cast and receive their script, giving actors plenty of time to get ready for the performance. The magnitude of the enemy force presented by procrastination cannot be underestimated.

Speaking of time management skills, discipline means saying no to over-socializing, whether in person or online. Partying is indeed a finite resource, and actors need to avoid over-doing it. You do not have to be the first one to leave Steak and Shake, or the party, but you definitely do not have to be the last one either. Social media is meant to enhance life, not replace it. Actors can in-

Present Laughter

crease productivity by unplugging to work on their performance pieces, or going to bed, so they can rest up in order to rehearse some more when they wake up. Discipline is actors committing to the creation of their own artistic works rather than serving as witnesses to the work of others. This means limiting time spent as an audience member to movies, television, online videos, and even plays. Yes, technically watching actors work in plays and movies can serve as research, but actors have a choice here: they can watch, or they can do. Why would actors want to sit and watch someone else act when they can get up and do it themselves? This does not suggest a ban on watching; it means limiting the time spent watching. Doing is better than watching because you learn more.

Discipline means saying yes to memorization. This is the one skill that all actors need, but the one that casting directors take for granted. It is assumed, if an actor is auditioning, that the actor can memorize scripts quickly. Directors do not sit in the house during auditions and think to themselves, "My, that actor is so talented. I wonder if they can memorize?" And yet that dreaded phrase, "Today you are off-book," seems to still send a bolt of terror through an actor's spine. It is like the actor has been cranking the handle on a jack-in-the-box, knows there is a jack that is going to pop up, and is still terrified when it pops up screaming "Off-book! Off-book!"

Most actors can memorize, but like, dude, memorization is hard. Still, the most practical exercise in acting class involves memorization. Locking yourself up in a room and solidly affixing a speech to your skull should be a source of pleasure, otherwise acting can turn into a source of pain.

One memorization technique is paraphrasing. Rephrasing the lines teaches ideas, not words, so that if the actor goes blank, they can still communicate the gist of the lines rather than standing before their partner, eyes bulging, beads of sweat trickling down their spine, mumbling, "I don't know what to say." If the actor knows enough to paraphrase, they can improvise their way out of a jam.

Then there is the mechanical connection: much beloved though hand-cramping, this involves writing out the lines repeatedly using longhand or typing. These repetitions force actors to chew each word thirty times, which aids in digestion, because people write slower than speak.

To me the best method is incrementalization. Let's say that you choose to use this technique, which involves learning a large speech in small increments. In incrementalization, actors learn the first sentence and repeat it aloud until they have it. Once that is done, they memorize the second sentence. Then they add the first one to the second. Then they add the third, and on and on until they've memorized all the lines. You can obfuscate the lines below the line you are studying using an index card to keep yourself from seeing the next line, which is like looking at the back of the puzzle book when you can't figure out the clue. The secret to success for memorization is for the actor to work it, work it, push it real good.

Whatever method the actor uses, memorization takes discipline. If the actor stumbles on lines during an audition, if the actor takes long, awkward pauses, or if they ask if they can start over, this is a sign to directors that maybe the actor has a poor work ethic. If the actor cannot get off-book for the audition, how will they ever get off-book for the performance? This question may cause the director not to cast the auditioning actor. When Sissy Spacek was in high school, her brother Robbie got cast in plays, but she never did. After Spacek won the Best Actress Oscar, her high school drama teacher explained to Spacek's mom why the teacher never cast Sissy: "Well, she didn't learn her lines!" (Spacek 2012, 81) Which just goes to show you cannot win an Oscar if you do not know your lines. Unless you are Marlon Brando.

Discipline is saying no to bad rehearsal and class etiquette. Good rehearsal etiquette means being on time and being nice to people. Good rehearsal etiquette means bringing a positive energy to everything and being enthusiastic about the team, the work, and the show. Good rehearsal etiquette means memorizing lines on schedule, remembering blocking and choreography, writing down notes from the director, and incorporating those notes into subsequent performances. In class, it means the student does the homework. Students should read the chapter before it is covered in class and do any assignments as directed. When performing exercises in class, students should commit to them, and not spend the whole class declaring that all the exercises are puerile and feckless.

Whether in class or a show, someone who does not want to be there, or someone who instigates backstage drama is a major downer. Unfortunately, almost every show and class seem to include at least one negative person. If actors and students go above and beyond to avoid negative attitudes and behavior, maybe they can contribute to a 100 percent positive environment, and wouldn't that be nice? Acting is hard enough without backstage conflict complicating things and making what should be fun into a torture fest.

In extreme situations, student actors may need to develop a show or class persona. Some may think this insincere, but since the Greek word for actors specifically referred to them as people who did not mean what they said, I am okay with that. If there is someone in the cast or class the student does not like, and working with them makes the student miserable, the student can create a version of themselves that gets along with that person, and when the student steps into class, they can become that version of themselves. Life and work are so much better when everyone gets along. This is only for extreme situations, but it is like the way people interact with different groups of people anyway. Take you, the student, for instance: you are one way with your family, you are another way at school, you are another way with your friends, and still another way at work. You are one way with a police officer and another way with your significant other, yet all these different personas are still only you. I suggest extending this practice to class and rehearsal so that interpersonal conflicts do not interfere with your art, work, and education.

Discipline is saying yes to focus and concentration. Alan Cumming (2014) says, "No matter what is going on in my real life, I know how to block it out when I am working. Whether I have had good news, bad news, am feeling hung over, joyful, sick, it's all part of the job description of an actor to know how to neutralize it all and become whatever the character needs to feel" (111). For class, this means focusing on the exercises, committing to the assignments, and doing the work. When two students partner up and go off to work on an assignment, like rehearsing a scene, it means working on the scene and not just hanging out. I have observed actors who were supposed to be rehearsing just sitting next to each other, one of them texting, the other browsing some website. This is procrastination, the actor's deadliest enemy.

In class and rehearsal, it means focusing on rehearsal. Sometimes rehearsal can get boring and repetitive. Temptation may lead the actor towards hijinks or pranks on their castmates, especially if they have been working together all semester. Resist the temptation and be productive.

Discipline means saying no to a detached attitude, one that waits for Superman to come and make the class or rehearsal worthwhile. When you are the student or the actor, you make the monologue performance, the exercise, the scene, or the play phenomenal. Alan Arkin (2011) runs improvisation workshops, and when he does, he resists when students expect him to deliver magic.

> *As the course developed, I found that in general the exercises I assembled were not wildly exciting. I didn't want to be Santa Claus, allowing the groups to fall into the trap of waiting for endless gifts and surprises from the teacher. That's the actor's disease. We're all waiting for the perfect part. For the perfect agent. The perfect play. The perfect scene partner. Then 'I can finally do some good work.' I wanted the group to feel that what they brought to the work was going to make the exercises exciting.*
> *(129–130)*

I cannot express the importance of this aspect of discipline—for actors to restrain themselves from using critiques of the material or their scene partners to keep them from doing good work.

I have witnessed actors working on Pulitzer Prize-winning material, like Steinbeck's *Of Mice and Men* and Lindsay-Abaire's *Rabbit Hole,* complain about the quality of the writing. I have witnessed actors, no matter with whom they were partnered, blame their scene partners for their own inability to do "good work" on the scene. I have witnessed students in class who indulge in a game I call the "Yeah buts." The student playing "Yeah but" calls every acting concept, regardless of source, pointless because they can conjure up the one exception that the theory fails to address as proof that the theory is twaddle. In response to an experienced, qualified, brilliant point, the "Yeah but" player will say, "Yeah, but what about blah blah blah?" Or during an exercise, giggle and complain instead of making a personal investment into the lesson. Resistance to the exercise is futile.

Perhaps this is a defense mechanism that stems from a fear of failure. As a student, do not fear the failure. Knowledge comes from failure. Class and rehearsal are where actors try things and fail, so that they do not make those mistakes during a performance in front of an audience. Defending against failure in class and rehearsal sets the actor up for failure in performance. Discipline and personal investment in the lesson, exercise, and rehearsal can save actors.

Discipline is saying yes to developing an interior life for the character and believing in imaginary circumstances rather than giving a strictly technical and exterior performance. It is not enough to pretend; the actor believes. This does not blur the line between fantasy and reality because it involves substituting reality for fantasy. Actors can believe in something that once was real. Figuring out something in your life that is analogous to what the character is thinking, feeling, or doing, and substituting your experience for that of the character, takes hard work, imagination, and self-mastery. That belief, though, can turn dry acting into sublime art.

Sissy Spacek provides an example of this type of substitution and inner life creation for the character when she tells the story of filming the shower scene in Stephen King's *Carrie*. Spacek (2012) says, "The water was warm, and I thought how Carrie would have enjoyed the feel of a hot shower, because she probably didn't get one at home. If you think of something, it will register on your face" (173). She then says that when the character sees the blood of her first period flowing, she used her imagination to substitute getting hit by a car to create the panic the character feels. This commitment to belief can help the actor create body language postures and micro-expressions on the character's face over which actors have no conscious control. Having an inner life for the character and experiences that can be imaginatively substituted can create acting on a subconscious level and make it real for the audience as well.

A horrible lie for people to hear is the one when they know they are being told a lie, and this is conjointly true for audiences. If the actor believes they are telling the truth, they can pass a lie detector test, because they believe they are not lying. Some audiences are a collective lie detector, looking for clues of deception in the actor's performance. The actor needs to believe. It is amazing what the mind can convince itself of: in a production of Rodney Ackland's *Absolute Hell*, Judi Dench (2010) played a big drinker. She describes the feeling of actual intoxication she achieved during performance. "In fact, although we were of course only drinking coloured water, I used to feel absolutely stotious afterwards. I can remember one night saying to Greg Hicks as we were on our hands and knees, 'How can we both be so drunk on coloured water?'" (150). When an actor can devote their whole self to a scene, it is an awesome feeling.

Present Laughter

The power of suggestion is awesome and staggering. When I was a junior in college, I was at a party and there was a gaggle of irritating freshmen who were being "naughty" for the first time. They asked our party host if he had any weed. The host went away for a moment and came back with a baggy filled with a leafy green substance. The freshmen went off, rolled some joints, and proceeded to get obnoxiously high. I knew the host was a teetotaler, so I asked him what was in the bag. He said it was catnip. But the freshmen believed they had killer weed, and I have never seen anyone so totally stoned as those young men believed they were.

The final aspect of discipline covered in this chapter—because the chapter has to end somewhere—is rejecting weak choices. Acting is all about making choices and then illustrating those choices to the audience. We discussed the dampening effect that fear of failure can have on actor training, and this is another aspect of that fear of failure. Say yes to interesting, bold, and imaginative choices. Do not just think of one thing, think of several and then choose the best of them. Brainstorming is a non-evaluative process of coming up with options when presented with a problem. If I am being non-evaluative, then I come up with something without worrying about whether it is good or not. I just come up with it. When brainstorming, if I come up with a list of possibilities, I can then go back and evaluate the things on my list and pick the best one. It is far easier to pick one good idea from a list of bad ones than it is to just come up with only one great idea.

Judi Dench (2010) describes it as such: "I think you have got to be prepared to make such ghastly mistakes; sometimes you make them onstage at the expense of the audience, you don't mean to but you just think, Oh, I'll try this and give it a whirl" (53). I will tell you from experience that an audience will forgive an actor just about anything except breaking character, and sometimes they like that too. One night during a production of *Das Barbecü*, my character was to point a prop revolver into the air and fire one shot. We were using a stage pistol that fired blanks. It was fully loaded, but when I fired the shot, the gun only clicked. I pulled the trigger again. Nothing. I pulled the trigger four more times to no avail, then pulled the gun down and looked it. Finally, I pointed the gun into the air and yelled "Bang!" The audience roared with laughter for what felt like minutes. The audience wants to go on the journey with the actor, they want you to succeed, and so they will go with you almost anywhere. Discipline means having the courage to make bold choices, to take chances, to live the magic.

Good choices come from specific information, which means the actor has used their mind's imagination to fully develop the character, which gives them numerous options from which to choose. I once played Shelly Levene in Mamet's *Glengarry Glen Ross*, and in the first scene Shelly is eating lunch with his boss in a Chinese restaurant. It is difficult to eat in a scene, and we were using real food in a realism production, so I really had to eat. An actor cannot shovel food into their mouth while speaking stage dialogue and be understood, so I decided, out of all the food on my plate, which foods Levene liked the most and which he liked the least, and this created an order as to how I would eat the food. My character was eating food he liked; I was not just an actor pretending to eat so I could lucidly say my lines. There is also a sense of desperate urgency in the scene, so I discovered how my character eats, in that he is a disgusting pig slob, otherwise he would have cared enough not to have this integral conversation during lunch. There were several spots where I sprayed chewed food on the table. My character did not care, except for once it was a chunk of a food he liked, so I picked it back up off the table and put it back in my mouth. The audience's reaction was priceless. They liked the choice.

Imagination, discipline, preparation, research, and analysis are all things that come from the mind of the actor. When an actor has a brilliant idea, we might say that they are inspired. Inspiration can be part of the imagination, but in my assessment of actor tools and actor training, I see inspiration as coming more from the actor's soul than from their mind. Our next chapter focuses on the soul, or spirit, of the actor.

Exercise 1

1. Scheduling: students need to create a detailed rehearsal schedule of when they will work on their monologues.
    A. Students should write out when and where the things in their lives that they must do take place: work, classes, family commitments, social engagements, etc.
    B. Students should designate rehearsal days and times.
    C. The professor should now hand out two blank month calendars to the class. Students should take these blank calendars and create a rehearsal schedule on paper just like a play production's rehearsal schedule or a class syllabus. The students should fill out two calendars.
    D. Students should keep one calendar schedule copy for themselves and give the professor the second copy.
    E. Students should stick to this schedule, and commit.
2. Circle of attention: class needs to arrange members in a circle formation.
    A. Volunteers with a memorized speech step into the circle—perhaps Monologue #1, another monologue, or song lyrics, something the volunteer has memorized already.
    B. Volunteer should recite the speech.
    C. Class makes noises and attempts to distract the volunteer while they recite the speech.
    D. The class should break into groups. Volunteers should take turns being the actor in the center of each group's circle while the rest of the group plays the part of the distractors.
3. Brainstorming.
    A. Professor writes a word on the board.
        a. Class responds to the word.
        b. Each member of the class should come up to the board individually and write one of their responses to the word.
        c. This creates a list of responses to the word.
        d. The class should next choose the best response out of the board's list.

B. Class should take out writing tools.
   a. Professor poses question to class (question TBD by professor or class). The question is:

   _____

   b. Each student brainstorms responses to the question, coming up with a list of possible responses. The student should write these responses down.
   c. Each student shares their response list with class. Once a student has shared their list, class picks best response from that student's list.
   d. Repeat sharing response list and selection of best response by class.
4. Inner life: what can the character be thinking while they say the words of the speech?
   A. Volunteer with Monologue #2, share the speech with the class. Read it aloud or recite if memorized.
   B. Class brainstorm possibilities.
   C. Class evaluate possibilities.
   D. Move on to other volunteers with their Monologue #2 and repeat.
5. Substitution: what are things from students' lives that they can substitute for the characters' things in their speeches?
   A. Volunteer read or recite, share Monologue #2 with the class.
   B. Class brainstorm possibilities.
   C. Class discuss possibilities.

Homework

1. Students should memorize Monologue #2.
2. Students should research their characters and record their research.
3. Students need to create the inner lives of their characters and record their choices.
4. Students need to create a list of substitute experiences for their monologues and record their choices.

Lesson 10
The Soul—That's the Spirit!

The third component, after the body and mind, that constitutes a good actor, is the soul. Alec Baldwin (2017), when speaking of acting, says, "Opportunities arrived to appreciate life's bounty, mysteries, truths, and heartbreak, to understand life on a higher plane. All of this while you play like a child again. And try to become immortal, like Marilyn Monroe or Elvis" (viii).

The actor must be an expert on human psychology and philosophy. Part of the urge of theatre, dating back to ancient Greece, is to tell stories that explain life's unexplainable things: Why are we here? What is the purpose of life? Who are we? What is the nature of the universe? These are the things Baldwin refers to when he talks about examining life on a higher plane.

You may be saying to yourself, "But Self, I do not believe in a soul," and that is fine; no one in class is required to believe anything. But acting is not just about the individual actor, it is about everyone collectively. Even if the actor does not believe, they may be playing a character who does, and actors play their characters without a wink, without commenting on the character's beliefs, without the actor saying to the audience through their portrayal of the character that the actor disagrees with the character. Actors understand their character's belief system.

If actors do not believe, they may be working with a director who does, and who has incorporated their belief into their conception of the play. Part of the actor's job is to convey the director's interpretation of the playwright's message to the audience. The playwright writes the script, the director analyzes the script and works with designers and actors to communicate that vision to the audience. If the actor disagrees with the director in matters of interpretation, it is the actor's duty to honor the director's interpretation, just as it is everyone's responsibility to honor the intentions of the playwright.

A large percentage of the world's population identifies themselves as religious. Theatre sometimes is dramatized philosophy, especially in the purer forms of tragedy and comedy. Here the term "soul" is not associated with religion. Many people say that they trust God but not people, and that they are not religious but spiritual. The term "soul" herein is used as a reference to things spiritual.

Sissy Spacek (2012) writes about the soul of the actor when she says,

> Even though we attended church every Sunday, my mother never bought into the traditional view that God was an external deity who ruled his kingdom from above. She always told me, "The kingdom of heaven is within," and "God is love," not restricted to any religion. A thumb-worn copy of Norman Vincent Peale's The Power of Positive Thinking was always nearby. She believed that what happens to you in this world isn't as important as how you respond to it. She could find God in the daily routines of life, and I must have absorbed these lessons from her, because it's what I believe. I find the divine in the ordinary, a miracle in every breath. And like her, I try to keep things simple. (36)

I believe in something. I do not know what it is. I believe it is not my responsibility to foist my beliefs on others. Acting class is never about delegating what is right and who is wrong. But there are acting styles that incorporate philosophy, a belief in the spiritual, so students can most benefit their actor training by taking what they can from this aspect of actor training and not let matters of faith keep them from mastering the art of acting. Judi Dench said it well when she quoted a speech Trevor Nunn delivered at her husband Michael's funeral. Nunn said, "I think it's only possible to discern the capacity for great acting in performers who themselves have a greatness of spirit, who have insight and burning moral passion that is transfiguring" (Dench 2010, 202). It can be said that spirituality is a consideration of not so much right and wrong, moral and immoral, but positive energy and negative energy. Or as George Lucas put it, the light side and the dark side. Or as Peter Griffin puts it, "Something, something . . . dark side."

Our bodies are finite, our souls—or the energies that animate our bodies—are infinite. The soul is that part of us that is in contact with powers greater than ourselves, the eternal existences. Our souls are part of our bodies, but separate. Sissy Spacek (2012), upon her brother's death, observed, "Once someone's spirit has left their body, it isn't them anymore. It's like the figures in a wax museum or after a cicada crawls out of its shell" (101). The movie *21 Grams*, starring two genuine method actors, Sean Penn and Benicio del Toro, takes its title from the work of scientist Dr. Duncan MacDougall. MacDougall, other than sounding like a character from *Macbeth,* conducted experiments in which he determined that, upon death, the body loses three-quarters of an ounce in weight. He cited this as evidence that a human soul weighs 21 grams.

Does it? I do not know, but Sidney Poitier wrote:

> There's a mystery to the relationship between life and an individual human personality, and I think the camera sees that mystery. The individual

> human personality has, bound up inside itself, a connection to all the wonders of the universe. When an artist is genuinely at work in his craft, he's more fully calling on those connections to the universal. (Poitier 2000, 140)

The universal is that connection to life, that connection to other people, that we feel when we are in the same room with them. There can be a connection between family members in their living room at home; there can likewise be a connection in a theater building between the people in the audience and the actors on the stage.

Our souls allow us to empathize with others, and without empathy, theatre would not be possible. Empathizing with people means actors can put themselves in another person's place and understand how they feel. In theatre, the audience empathizes with the characters, empathetically bonding with them and vicariously experiencing the character's emotional journey. In some instances, audience members project themselves into the character, and it is like the actions of the play are happening to them.

For actors, empathy means being able to connect with the audience and to bond with the character's feelings. Alec Baldwin (2017) puts it this way, discussing his own instinctual ability: "I realized I had an above-average empathy for other people's feelings . . . I could understand other people, get inside them, better than most. I began to think that maybe this acting idea wasn't such a bad decision after all" (50).

The actor gets inside the character, understands how the character feels about things, and sees things as the character sees them. The actor empathizes with the character, the audience empathizes with the actor playing the character, and this process of sharing feelings is the heart of good acting. The actor understands a vast swath of humanity. Alan Arkin (2011) said:

> In some deep place I always believed that what everyone else was feeling or doing, whether it be an act of heroism or cowardice or compassion or greed or villainy or anything in between, whatever the characters were going through emotionally was possible for me. I sensed that the entire range of emotions possessed by any human being was universal and accessible to everyone. (9)

Lt. Joe Kenda on *Homicide Hunter,* a documentary crime television show, once opined in an episode that one thing spending decades as a homicide detective had taught him is that anyone is capable of everything. Actors embrace that philosophy, otherwise they spend time deciding what the character would or wouldn't do, which effectively puts the character in a cage. Some actors, like Marlon Brando, believe it is the actor's responsibility to experience everything in life without making moral judgments because then the actor has more personal experience to draw from and more empathy with which to connect to humanity's universal aspects.

The soul is where talent comes from, the gifts and abilities we are born with, not something learned but something for which we have a natural affinity. Talent often manifests at an early age for actors as a strong desire to perform. Sissy Spacek (2012) writes, "My parents had a full-length mirror on their closet door, and I loved to sit in front of it and read aloud to myself. I would give all of the characters different voices and imagine how they would behave in the stories. I might not have known it then, but this could have been the dawn of my acting career" (83).

Spacek started at an early age, as did I. I began my education at Huxford Elementary, nestled between forests, cotton fields, and soybean fields in rural Escambia County, Alabama, right next to the pole mill. There were no music or drama programs offered to students under grade seven, but that did not stop me. My parents had given me a hardcover collection of *Peanuts* comic strips for Christmas one year in the early 1970s. I went through the books making check marks next to the strips that I thought, when compiled, would make a good script for a play starring me as Charlie Brown. It was a close call—I desperately wanted to play Snoopy as well, but eventually the round-headed kid won out. It proved to be a wasted struggle, as I could get no one interested in doing the show with me. Hard to believe there was a scarcity of future theatre majors in rural Alabama in the 1970s, I know. My *Peanuts* play may never have been realized, but it primed my hunger for performance art, and I was ready when I got to middle school and signed up first for chorus and then in junior high, drama class!

Actors can tell that they have talent when they have a strong urge to perform at an early age. Talent rearing its head creates that urge. Spacek (2012) describes going to the theatre at an early age and being amazed at the beauty of the place.

> And it got even better when we took our seats in the auditorium. The music started up, and out marched the Coquettes. As soon as I saw them on that stage, boys and girls turning their batons, dressed up in shimmery silver cowboy outfits, hats, and white majorette boots, I knew show business was for me. I could do that, I thought. I should be up there. (68)

My first exposure to live theatre inspired in me a similar reaction. Roy Rogers and Dale Evans, then well into senior citizenhood, brought their show to Huxford Elementary School. Seeing them perform live deeply impressed me. I had been exposed to Roy and Dale from birth as my father was a huge fan of westerns; if one was on television, that was what we were watching. This was in the days of television antennas, when there were only three channels, and usually only one television in the house that the viewer had to get up and walk to in order to change the channel. It was Roy Rogers and Dale Evans that had inspired me to create my stage play adapted from *Peanuts* that never actually premiered anywhere.

Jesus Christ Superstar

If, as a small child, you are deeply moved when you first see live entertainment, that may be the theatre bug chomping down on you. This is your natural born talent signaling to you its presence and that onstage is where you need to live your life. Amy Poehler (2014) puts it this way: "Creativity is connected to your passion, that light inside you that drives you. That joy that comes when you do something you love. That small voice that tells you, 'I like this. Do this again. You are good at it. Keep going.' That is the juicy stuff that lubricates our lives and helps us feel less alone in the world" (222). Notice she does not say anything about other people telling her that she is good; this affirmation is coming from herself. Talent is without ego; it recognizes itself. Beauty is not the only thing in the eye of the beholder. If your art speaks to you, then chances are it will speak to others. If at first the student actor does not get affirmation from others, the student needs to keep working. The students will grow in their abilities over time and will find their audience. You can get there from here!

But student actors cannot get there with just talent, which is the reason for the existence of classes like this one. Sidney Poitier (2000) explains why talent alone is not enough. "I always knew that first-rate actors had exceptional gifts, but I also knew that an exceptional gift, in and of itself, didn't necessarily a first-rate actor make. It was essential that the actor's gift be subject to a technique, a learned procedure, a discipline, in order for him to constantly function at close to his best" (143). Thus, the need for actor training programs around the world.

Talent comes from the soul, a gift with which people are born, perhaps from a higher power if they are into that. The soul's most important province is as the home of human emotions. Our body is how we communicate and perform actions in the physical world; our mind is the home of logic and our intellect. Our soul is the seat of our emotions. Alan Arkin (2011), when describing his "heart" in the following passage, is speaking of what I refer to as the soul, as in heart and soul, which are synonymous. "The heart, from a metaphysical standpoint, is just what you would expect it to be, a place of love and connection and vulnerability" (80).

An actor who can create genuine emotional reactions onstage is a wonderful thing, but how do we do that? Sidney Poitier had some advice for actors who want to create emotional reactions onstage or on camera, as if it were real life. "He goes to his sense memory. He goes deep inside himself into a place where all his individual sense memories are stored, and that place then connects him with the universe." He refers to a network of instincts that drive humanity. All the actor's life is in their sense memory even if it is not available to their conscious mind. "But in acting, a creative moment requires that the actor enter there. And the camera sees that contact with the sense memory. So what it picks up is something that's almost indescribable. Some people call it *presence*, while others say the camera *likes* the actor. Whatever label we apply, the camera sees *something*; it just simply sees it." Poitier goes on to say, "Even when there are no lines being said, you know something's going on in that mind, in that soul. . . . That's because he's entering that creative place. Or maybe not so much *entering* it as being *receptive* to it" (Poitier 2000, 141–142). However, not every actor is as emotionally sensitive as what Poitier describes here, even actors who are considered great. And even those actors who can tap into genuine emotion cannot do it 100 percent of the time. If a stage actor is employed in a long run with a show, and one night the actor is not feeling it, the actor still does the show, and the seventy-fourth audience deserves the same great performance the actor gave to the third audience.

Theatre is magic, but magic takes hard work. Those actors who can tap freely into their emotions and use them liberally are often referred to as "method actors," whereas those who "fake it" are known as technical actors. Perhaps the most famous example of the differences between the two approaches is said to have occurred during the filming of the movie *Marathon Man,* between method actor Dustin Hoffman and technical actor Sir Laurence Olivier. Michael Simkins tells the story in an article for *The Guardian.*

> *Dustin Hoffman has long been known as one of method acting's most earnest exponents. A showbiz story involves his collaboration with Laurence Olivier on the 1976 film* Marathon Man. *Upon being asked by his co-star how a previous scene had gone, one in which Hoffman's character*

has supposedly stayed up for three days, Hoffman admitted that he too had not slept for 72 hours to achieve emotional verisimilitude. "My dear boy," replied Olivier smoothly, "why don't you just try acting?" (Simkins 2016, 1)

Simkins goes on to laud English actors and their "ability to replicate emotion on demand."

Jesus Christ Superstar

It is not necessary, although it is nice, that the actor feel anything. Rather, it is important that the people in the audience feel something. For this to happen, the actor needs to appear to be feeling something; therefore, actors play actions, not emotions. Ironically, performing actions is a gateway to creating genuine emotional reactions instead of pretend emotions. If actors perform the physical actions people associate with an emotion, their sense recall will remember that emotion, and performing that action will to some extent recreate that emotion inside the actors. One way to remember the concept is this:

Motion creates *E*-motion

See what I did there? By adding the letter "e" to motion, we create the new word, "emotion." Motion comes first, which creates the emotion.

If an actor does not feel the desired emotion, the actor performs an action, which creates the spark of that emotion, and the actor then fans that spark into a full-blown flame. If the actor does not feel it, they are still performing the action, and the show, as it ever must, goes on. You either feel it or you do not; hopefully you feel it. Gene Wilder (2005) put it this way when he wrote:

> Stanislavski's system, or "method" as it's now usually referred to, just boils down to finding logical behavior in a situation and then using your own real emotions as you create your part. Strasberg taught many techniques to get to these emotions—I use some of them and I don't use others—but truly looking and truly listening has always been the heart and soul of any good actor's technique. (82)

Truly looking and listening as the character are actions. Performing actions creates emotional reactions. If actors are truly looking at sets, props, lights, costumes and their acting partners, actors will have genuine emotional reactions to what they are doing, their actions. If they are truly listening, this means their characters are listening to the other characters for openings and strategies that they can use to achieve their objectives. Active listening to the other characters' vocal actions is a double character action actors perform and therefore is twice as powerful a source for generating emotions.

A technique actors can use for either replicating or generating emotional responses involves visualization and a color scheme that defines certain emotional reactions by association with a particular color. Actors can create a color scheme that identifies an emotion, and then pick a color that represents that emotion for them. Students in this class, based on analysis of the lines and actions of the character, can determine what emotions the character is going through. When the actor plays that segment, they can visualize its color in their head, and that will help generate that emotion in their performance. This can take a performance out of Dorothy's gray Kansas into colorful Oz, to use a stereotypical metaphor that is stereotypical because it is true.

Diverse colors can mean different things to sundry people, especially people of heterogeneous cultural backgrounds. Black and white, for instance, can mean the exact opposite to a person from the United States of America than it does to a person from China, so color schemes are subjective and not an exact science. Ultimately, students pick the color that conjures that emotion for them. To me, for instance:

RED = passion or anger

BLUE = sadness or serenity

GREEN = greed or envy

ORANGE = healthy or optimistic

YELLOW = warm or comfortable

PINK = love

PURPLE = superiority or smugness

BLACK = evil

WHITE = purity or coldness

GREY = confusion or uncertainty

BROWN = disappointment or misery

Once students have a color scheme, or a set of colors with a table of concomitant emotions, students may get highlighters, colored pencils, or see-through markers for each color. Students can then analyze their monologue or scene, breaking it into emotional beats. Students can take the highlighters or markers and paint each section of the speech in its requisite color. When they do so, they can chart the character's emotional journey sans words.

Jesus Christ Superstar

When an actor performs an emotional beat, they can visualize that color in their mind. Visualizing the color may help actors feel in-depth emotions. Scoring a script in color is like turning the script into the equivalent of sheet music, making the printed speech to eyes as audible music is to ears. Adolphe Appia's use of light came from his belief that light is to the eye as music is to the ear, and he believed in the concept of painting with light to create an effective, unified mise-en-scène. Much of his theories concern not only light and darkness, but the use of colored light. Applying Appia's work from musical scores to an actor's script, painting the script with colors can aid actors in the creation of genuine emotions on stage. Those who desire to know more about Appia's work can read about his theories in his books, *The Staging of Wagner's Musical Dramas*, *Music and Stage Setting*, and *The Work of Living Art*.

When an actor feels real emotions during a performance, it is one of the most rewarding feelings they can ever have. This enables actors to give inspired performances. Inspiration, like talent and emotion, comes from the soul. Alan Arkin (2011) describes arduously preparing for a role and getting to a point where he *becomes* the character; he is not replicating actions and emotions, they are genuine. "When I walked onto the stage, it was as if the character told me to get out of the way and mind my own business." He describes it as an out-of-body experience. "For those few moments I was living in a state of grace. It was a place where nothing could go wrong" (24). But you can only get in this zone through hard work: ". . . it only seems to take place with those who are deeply devoted to the art or sport or work in which it is occurring" (26).

Exercise 1

1. As a class, students create a list of emotions that actors may need to convey over a wide variety of roles.
    A. The class should break into groups. Each group should decide on a color that represents each emotion. In the case of disagreement, members of the group can argue their positions, then allow the group to vote. For the purposes of this exercise, compromise. Individual actors can go back to their individual charts on their own once the exercise is over.
    B. As a class, discuss each group's color chart and come to a consensus decision that establishes one color-emotion representation chart for this class, this semester. Choices will again be discussed and in cases where strong arguments are made for various colors to represent the same emotion, majority vote will decide the one color. For this class, there can be only one!

Exercise 2

1. Volunteers, one at a time, take the stage and share their Monologue #2 with the class. Volunteers may read it if necessary or recite from memory.
2. Class should discuss each monologue after each performance.
    A. Identify possible emotions represented in various places of the monologue.
    B. Chart the emotional journey of the speech.

Exercise 3

1. The class should experience an episode of guided meditation, perhaps the YouTube video, "Let Go of Anxiety, Fear and Worries: A Guided Meditation > Harmony, Inner Peace & Emotional Healing," or another similar video.
2. Alternatively, professors can lead the class in guided meditation using their own session material.

Exercise 4

1. The class needs to perform a series of physical actions. These actions are identified in the next step of the exercise. After the performance of each action, the class should discuss and identify the primary emotion each action generates in each student.
2. Actions: the professor or class leader calls out the action. The class performs the action. Then the class discusses the action, decides what emotion it creates, before the professor moves on to calling out the next action. Repeat procedure for all actions.

   A. Punch: class should try a variety of punches and punch intensities.

   B. Kick: class should try a bunch of kicks with varying intensities.

   C. Wave.

   D. Bow.

   E. Curtsy.

   F. Run.

   G. Do jumping jacks.

   H. Stab.

   I. Shoot.

   J. Shove someone back by using "The Force."

   K. Call down the lightning with your magic hands.

   L. Shoot someone with your laser palm.

   M. Squat.

   N. Kneel.

   O. Clasp hands as though in deep thought or prayer.

   P. Turn to a classmate and shake hands.

   Q. Turn to a classmate and hug.

   R. Kiss an invisible, intangible someone; not a classmate, an imaginary someone. Pretend you have a scene partner, like your character in a monologue is kissing someone.

Homework

1. Student actors should do an emotion-beat analysis of their Monologue #2.
2. Student actors should get various colored highlighters or markers that correspond to their color trajectory.
3. On a printed copy of their monologue, student actors should paint each emotional beat with its corresponding color, creating an emotional score for their Monologue #2.

Lesson 11
Audition Technique
How to Do That Thing You Do

The audition is the theatrical job interview, and it comes with all the stress of a normal job interview, only worse. In the real world, when someone goes to a job interview, the interviewer knows exactly what qualities they are looking for in a candidate. Directors often do not know what they are looking for until they see it. Sometimes directors may even think they know exactly what they want but when they see it decide that they were wrong, or they see something else and think maybe that will be better. As the auditioning actor, you are not really sure what the director wants, but you hope that they see it in you.

Often the actor is not even auditioning for the part, the actor is auditioning for a callback. A callback is a follow-up audition for the purpose of the director seeing actors do their audition piece again, or read something else, or do an improvisation, or perform another monologue, or sing a different song, or perform an interpretive dance, or escape from a straitjacket, what have you. Personally, I do not like callbacks. I was the kind of actor who said, "Callback? I already auditioned for this play once, weren't you paying attention the first time?" But there are directors who insist on callbacks, so auditioning actors need to prepare for that process.

Actors can help themselves in the hiring process by showing that they are receptive to direction and have the skill set to play any part. Receptive actors are teachable and have a positive attitude towards the collaborative process. Actors show casting directors that hiring the actor is a good choice.

Throughout my career I have had choreographers, music directors, associate directors, and assistant directors raise their eyebrows at some of my casting choices, only to express by opening night that I had made perfect casting choices. I believe theatre is magic, and sometimes in casting I just trust my gut. That said, I believe in gender blind, color blind, and age blind casting. *Hamilton* was a lovely thing to see when it opened, as was the reception to its casting. However, casting in theatre will remain less inclusive if producers believe audiences will reject perceived outré casting choices. Upon Daniel Craig's decision to leave the James Bond film franchise, there were entertainment media reports of the possibility of casting a person of color in the Bond role. This caused a furor in certain corners of fandom for the character, and this furor reinforces the perception that "traditional casting" days may not be quite over yet. Actors are still auditioning for characters that the writer, director, producer, or all of the above believe the actor looks like. It's still typecasting.

Is auditioning fun? It can be, but there are actors who say no. Whether the actor likes auditioning or not, it is how actors get into plays. Auditions are necessary. Actors cannot control that. All they can do is control how they react to the audition experience. The same is true of life: you can choose to hate life, or you can choose to love life, it is actor's choice.

There are reasons for dreading and hating auditions, to be sure. Even the greatest actors, at least at the start of their careers, had to audition. Robert DeNiro said of auditions, "I didn't have a problem with rejection because when you go into an audition you're rejected already. There are hundreds of other actors. You're behind the eight ball when you go in" (Levy 2014, 66). He is referring to the air of desperation at auditions. Everybody wants the part, but there are only a few parts and a plethora of actors, so there are going to be plenty of broken hearts. It is simple math. Granted, theatre majors are often bad at math, but even I, a lifetime theatre major, get that.

The stress can cause you to act out. Amy Poehler (2014) shares:

> *I was never great in auditions. When I was nervous I would often underprepare and act too cool for school. I would try to reject them before they rejected me, which was confusing since I had decided to audition and acted angry to be there. I remember one particular time I auditioned for the Coen Brothers. I realized I was doing a pretty shitty job and I overcompensated by also acting like a dick. (219)*

Which brings up a good point: do not be a jerk. No matter how talented the auditioning actor is, there are going to be a dozen people behind them who are also talented but not jerks. No one chooses to work with a cretin when they could work with nice people instead.

In the audition, actors are selling themselves, but they cannot let that need to sell get in the way of showing their acting abilities. Alan Arkin (2011) describes how he, as a director, approaches this dichotomy by instructing auditioning actors to do it again, once they have had an initial foray, but to "try it again without the acting." Doing this "invariably makes the actor breathe a sigh of relief and smile as if they are saying, 'You mean you actually want me to do what I was *trained* to do? What I *enjoy* doing? I can just *play* the part? I don't have to *sell* the part?' I have them go back and do the scene again, and it is invariably looser, more personal, and infinitely more interesting" (111). While actors do want to relax, have fun, and reduce tension, they cannot completely lose track of the fact that they are up there trying to show judges why they should pick them in particular and not someone else. Despite all the competition, actors' chances of getting cast are much better than winning the lottery, because actors do have some control over their fate by how they prepare. Acting I is here to help student actors on that journey. Students need to do the following in this class for their second and third audition monologues.

The Wedding Singer

In this class, we will either have a sign-up sheet ahead of time for actors to select the time slot and performance order they prefer, or we may call for volunteers. If no one wishes to volunteer, the professor can call names in random order. Spoiler alert: all people with names will have to act that day. However it happens, once your name is called, you should take the performance space with energy and enthusiasm. If, when your name is called, you say, "Dang it," or "Crap," or groan "Oh no," or exasperatedly moan, "I knew it," that tells your audience, quite literally, that you do not want to perform. You condition your audience—the rest of the class and your professor—to not enjoy your performance. It is like going to see a singer, or a stand-up comic, and before the show they announce, "I'm going to do my thing now, I'm sorry, please forgive me." Or you place an order at a restaurant and the waiter says, "That's probably going to taste like crap, but I'll go get it for you."

Actors who do this are telling the audience not to expect quality, that the performance is going to be lousy. They are telling audiences to reject them, perhaps out of fear that audiences might reject them. If the actor brings negative energy into their performance space, they reduce their chances for a positive outcome. Actors can be optimistic and bring positivity to their playing. After all, it is supposed to be fun, actors and audiences are supposed to enjoy their time together. If the actors screw up, nobody dies, even in a tragedy.

Judi Dench discusses the need to lighten up and have positive energy when she compares Pierce Brosnan's portrayal of James Bond to that of Daniel Craig. She observes that "Both are very good actors with an enormous sense of humour, and that is really important. I think you have got to be a bit of self-deprecating as Bond; if you take yourself too seriously in it, or in anything, really, it isn't good" (Dench 2010, 218). If an actor projects a cloud of doom while performing, their audience will pick up on it. If the actor is miserable, the audience is miserable. Actors who enjoy their performance encourage the audience to enjoy it with them.

Dench discusses this phenomenon of shared positive energy when she speaks of crowd reactions to the 2010 revival of *A Midsummer Night's Dream*. At a reception after one performance, she says, "Somebody said to me, 'Oh, you all look as if you are having such fun.' I thought that proved that when we all enjoy each other's company it transmits itself to an audience. It is not that we are going out there thinking what fun we are all having, but doing it to convey this glorious story" (Dench 2010, 236). So how about that? In this class, please try to enjoy yourself. Enjoy the opportunity to perform. When called to do so, say to yourself, "Self! I love acting! Therefore, I am here! This is wonderful!" Then take the space and have a good time.

Students should introduce themselves and their material to the class. A movie slate is that clapper board thing that someone holds before the camera at the start of a scene that identifies it so that the movie director and editor know which scene they are looking at, whether or not it goes in the final cut, and where it fits in the film's chronology. The information that an actor speaks before they perform their audition monologue is also called a slate. It is a verbal, spoken slate only; you do not need an actual movie slate, or to clap your hands or anything. For this class, you stand at performance ready, smile, and tell us your name and what you are performing. For instance, "Hi, I'm Rodney Whatley and I'll be doing Willy Loman from *Death of a Salesman*." Immediately after the slate, take your starting position, get into character, and go!

Once you have finished the monologue, you need a proper ending. Please do not say "Scene" or some variation of this. Just drop character, stand up straight, smile, say thank you, take a bow, and leave the performance space.

The goal of this class is to help prepare students so that they can successfully audition for plays or acting companies. When auditioning for community theatre productions, admittance to a college, university or acting school, scholarships, parts in educational theatre productions, or professional theatre jobs, there are some things that are universal and integral to the success of student actors.

The first thing auditioning actors need to do is to prepare well ahead of time. Even if it is a long drive, memorizing the material while in transit is not recommended. Actors should pick their audition pieces well in advance and rehearse them until they are sick of them. If it is a serious piece, by the time the actor is called up, they should be more familiar with the speech than the person who wrote it. If it is a comedic piece, the actor should have forgotten that when they first read the thing, they thought it was funny. If laughter comes, it should be a complete surprise, but the actor still needs to stay in character.

The Wedding Singer

Actors should always arrive early for the audition; do not arrive at the location at the last minute. Be there ready and waiting when the audition process begins. If possible, familiarize yourself with the location site ahead of time so that when you get there on the day, you are not freaking out and running around going, "Where do I go? Where do I go? What do I do? Is this the building? What floor is it on? What room is it in?" Part of this is to show that you are thoughtful, considerate, prompt, and professional. A big part of this, though, is so that this kind of uncertainty and stress does not negatively impact your attitude and actual performance. You need to be pleasant, relaxed, and composed, and that will not happen if you are lost, anxious, and confused.

A fellow director of mine taught me the phrase, "Early is on time, on time is late, late is you're fired." What late says in an audition situation is that the actor cannot take direction. The instructions for the audition, including location and time, are the equivalent of notes from the director on how to audition. Failure to follow them sends the message that the actor may be talented, but they will be difficult to work with because they cannot take direction.

The audition starts when the actor walks into the room, theater, or wherever the audition is being held. To be clear: it does not start when you are on the stage after you have said your slate. Your audition begins once you enter the room and you can be seen and heard. These are the things being judged immediately:

- Your appearance—to some extent you are being typed by your physicality.
- Your raiment—it is amazing how much wardrobe says about the person, so be sure you know what message you are communicating and if it is the message you intend.
- How you move and speak—are you confident and assured or self-doubting and shaky?
- How you interact with others—do you play well with hoi polloi or are you socially uncomfortable, prickly, or a misanthrope?
- Your level of professionalism and experience—does it look like you have done this before, do you know what you are doing, or is this your first rodeo?

How you interact with others is crucial. The casting directors are looking to put people together for the rehearsal period of the show and then for the run of the show, which can encompass a long time. The longest I was ever with one acting company was fifteen months, and this was an extremely intense shared experience in which everyone in the company got to know each other intimately. Be kind, be courteous, be nice, be someone other people will want to be around.

Being directable is fundamental. If an actor cannot or will not take direction, chances are directors, whose job it is to give actors directions, will not want to work with that actor. In addition to any instructions the organization gives you ahead of time, pay close attention to any instructions given to you once on site. Digesting these and successfully following them when others fail to do so is an opportunity to show your intelligence and competence.

I remember at a Southeastern Theatre Conference audition once, my pod of thirty had been given instructions on what to do once we left the green room, what to do backstage, and how to exit stage left once we were done with the audition. My attention wandered and I missed the dire warning about needing to exit via the downstage leg stage left. I exited mid-stage and could not get to the door, so I was trapped backstage until the actor after me had finished and then I had to awkwardly join them as they exited correctly. I did it with the biggest grin I could muster, and there was some laughter at my error, but they were laughing at me, not with me.

The auditioning actor's dress and appearance are a vital set of factors. Please do take care of personal hygiene. Bathe, deodorize, and avoid heavy cologne or perfume. Utilize only light makeup and pay professional but not obsessive attention to your hair. Facial hair, if any, should be well-trimmed. Brushed teeth and fresh breath are both good ideas. Get some rest so you do not look exhausted, and do not show up with a hangover, or smelling of smoke. Drinking and smoking are bad, mmkay?

An audition is a job interview, so dressing at least business casual is recommended. Overly formal attire may restrict your movements and may detract from your image of accessibility. Clothing choices will never please everyone: no matter what color you choose, it is going to be someone's favorite color and the color someone else loathes more than anything. You can wear stripes, polka dots, triangles, or plaid—somebody is going to like it and somebody else is going to hate it. The best you can do is to wear something that is not falling apart, bespeaks professionalism, is conducive to movement, reasonably comfortable, and supports you without distracting from you.

There is some argument as to whether one should wear a costume or something that is suggestive of a costume at an audition. Gene Wilder always wore costumes to his auditions, but most guidelines for college, university, and professional auditions advise against it. I will say this: it marks you as an eccentric when you wear a costume to an audition. At university, after I transferred in from a two-year school, I attended my first audition wearing a hooded cape. I had taken a passage from Terry Brooks's 1982 fantasy novel, *The Elfstones of Shannara*, and adapted it into a monologue. Putting on my cloak, I looked like Luke Skywalker approaching Jabba the Hutt in *Return of the Jedi*. I did not talk to anyone all night, just sat silently in the back being weird and shunned. I loved it. For some reason I got cast in the show. Okay, I know the reason: the director was a lunatic and recognized me as like-minded and so cast me. I got lucky. You cannot count on that happening. Not all directors are insane, just like not all old men yell "Get off my lawn!" at children. By the way, can you, you know, get off my lawn? Thanks.

Some organizations warn against wearing all black for auditions, as they perceive that to be the equivalent of a costume. There is no science to picking the right outfit. Pick something that you feel good in, because if you hate what you are wearing, some of that misery will transmit to the judges, even if only on a subconscious level.

When I was an undergraduate, I got competitive scholarships, first to a two-year school, and then to a wonderful four-year institution. I got a graduate assistantship for my MFA, and for my PhD studies I was awarded both teaching and research assistantships. I have also auditioned at SETC and Midwest Theatre Conference and gotten employment contracts, and over the years had the pleasure of many professional and amateur auditions in addition to the scores of auditions for college productions during my eleven years as a student sitting in classrooms. The most valuable lesson I have learned is that you should do as much research on the audition as possible, so you improve your chances of giving them what they want. Check their website. Read the audition notice. Familiarize yourself with the rules. If you have any questions, and there is a phone number or an email address, submit an inquiry or call for help.

In addition to not going into the audition blind, you should be an expert on your audition material. It can be truly embarrassing if, during an interview, the auditor asks you a question and you do not know the answer. If they ask you what play your monologue is from, you should know. You should at least know the spark notes about it. If they ask you about your character, you should be able to discuss it. If you do not know the answer, avoid faking it or lying because if they ask about provable facts, you will look foolish. With a little investigation, they may prove that you are ignorant, dishonest, or both. Just tell them you do not know now, but that you are willing to learn and happy to get back with them at their convenience. But the best thing is to know the material.

Once when I auditioned at SETC, I got several callbacks, and in one of the interviews one of the first questions they asked

The Wedding Singer

was, "Do you have another monologue you can do for us?" Of course the answer was yes. One monologue is never enough; a good actor plying the boards needs at least four contrasting monologues ready to go forthwith.

There are two different ways one may contrast: genre and chronology. Genre is the French word for category, or type, and the two major genres are comedy and tragedy. Chronology refers to time, so you need something old or classic, and something new or contemporary. "New" generally refers to the work of Henrik Ibsen and the advent of realism all the way up to contemporary works. "Contemporary" refers to works created within the last twenty years. You need one classic serious, one classic funny, one modern serious, and one modern funny monologue.

When I was on the circuit, I always had five monologues; the fifth one was one I had written for myself. One year in a callback, they asked me after each monologue if I had another monologue I could show them. If possible, the actor wants to be able to say yes in these interviews, so I kept doling out the monologues until I had done all five. I did not know what I was going to do if they asked for another one, but thank goodness they did not.

Being an expert on your material also means having every aspect of your performance planned and rehearsed. Each monologue needs to have blocking and gestures planned and rehearsed until they seem natural, spontaneous, and supportive of the words, illustrating them without distracting from them. Do not make up blocking and gestures as you go. Improvisation has its place, but it is not in an audition for a scripted performance where you are performing a memorized monologue.

If an actor attempts to make up blocking and gestures on the spot, they have no idea what they are going to get, how it is going to look, or what it is going to say to the audience, even if it is an audience of one. Auditors, directors, casting directors, agents, and professors are, after all, only that: an audience.

Another major danger to improvised movements is that they may lack purpose. Aimless movement without purpose is distracting, and for a knowledgeable audience member, frustrating, as it detracts from the art's message. What you want is the illusion of the first time when you perform, not the actual first time.

It would be wise to incorporate all the lessons of the previous chapters, especially the ones on the body, the mind, and the soul.

When it comes to selecting your performance pieces, pick something that appeals to you and something that suits you. It needs to appeal to you because you are entering a long-term relationship with it. You may be with it for life. And it should be something that suits you, that shows you in a good light, a light that says, "Cast me, hire me!" Pick something that is in your comfort zone or speaks to your strengths as a performer. The audition is where the actor shows their strengths, not their weaknesses.

Pick something that has emotional richness and displays emotional variety. You do not want a piece that is all one color; you want a conglomeration of iridescence. As a senior undergraduate, I went to my first state screening for SETC. I had picked a monologue about an anthropomorphized rat in his rat hole complaining about how horrible it was to be a rat. I thought it was hilarious and whenever I played it, I got a lot of laughs. The three-judge panel enjoyed the performance and passed me on to SETC, but one of them warned me that it was one-note, all anger, and all red. They said, "Anger is the easiest emotion for an actor to play, don't be lazy, look for opportunities to play the unexpected."

I did, and that has led me to the belief that no speech is ever emotionally unified. Even in the saddest, most serious piece, look for a moment of humor, even if it is sarcastic or bemused. The funniest speech needs a twinkling of dusk. The only way to know you are in the dark is if you can see some light, and you need light in order to cast a shadow.

The one thing you can be sure of as an actor, outside of this classroom, is that if you audition, you will face at some time rejection and failure. In this class, students are not graded on talent; students are graded on the work. Students who do the work do not have to worry about their grades.

In the real world, there are only so many parts and there is an abundance of actors. Some actors might feel that if someone else got the part and they got rejected, then there are too many actors. Some actors might feel that we need to get rid of just enough actors until the part goes to them, and at that point there will be just the right number of actors.

It is easy to tell others to not take it personally, but rejection feels personal, even when the person rejecting the actor is a complete stranger. Every auditioning actor knows they should be the one playing the part. How many actors does it take to screw in a light bulb? Five: one to do it and four to say, "I could do that better." The simple truth is that no one gets cast 100 percent of the time. Auditioning is good training, though, because it trains actors to deal with failure.

Alec Baldwin (2017) writes of handling failure even when the actor wins the audition. "The excitement of scoring my job as an actor comes with that dichotomy. The movie bombs, the play closes, or the TV show is cancelled, and your joy is quickly replaced by disappointment. But you try to remember that it's not your fault. At least, not entirely. Finding an audience is a difficult task and failure is the norm" (90). If you are not cast at auditions, it is not your fault. You cannot control who the director picks, so do not fret over it. All you can do is your best; the rest is out of your hands.

There is a debate, however: if it is not your fault, is it the fault of the other actors? In other words, is acting a competition? Some say that acting is a contact sport, a competitive form of art, as they view the audition process like a talent show. Gabrielle Union (2017) argues that it is a competition when she writes, "There's always someone bigger, badder, better. Don't save your best for when you think the material calls for it. Always bring your full potential to every take, and be on top of your job, or they will replace you" (125). She speaks from decades of experience in the movie and television industry, where no one's job is safe.

Judi Dench is of the opposing school of thought. She writes that in school she was taught "to do it well but not to compete," not only in sports but also in the arts. Despite her expressed fondness for winning awards, she disapproves of them, "because you can't really award prizes for acting. . . . Acting is such a personal, imperfect kind of art" (Dench 2010, 7).

Fine sentiments, if confusing, because in sports, there is competition with clear winners and losers. Every four years, the world stops to watch the Olympics, and every year in the dead of winter America sits down to watch the Super Bowl, or at least to see which company has the best commercial, yet another form of competition and one that includes actors in those commercials.

All the actors who audition do not get a participation trophy, or role—you either get cast or you go home. And despite Dame Judi's protestations that you cannot give out awards for acting, every year people flock to the Tony's, the Golden Globes, the Oscars, and more. So yes, obviously, you can award prizes for acting.

Alan Arkin (2011) sides with Dame Judi. He describes the atmosphere he strives to create when he is teaching an improvisation workshop, where he tries to get the participants to see themselves as a unified group. "This is rarely taught in acting classes, where I often find a subtle, unstated sense of competition between actors. In classes as well as in much theatre and film work, I often feel the vibes of people being extremely nice to each other in order to hide an underlying jockeying for position. I want to counteract that impulse here" (138). It is good when you can achieve that unity. It would be nice if the lion and the lamb could play together, but in the real jungle, the lion eventually is going to get hungry. For professional actors, we live in a capitalistic society, so if you do not get cast, you do not eat, and you sleep outside. It is a jungle out there for actors. And if they could, your house cats would eat you.

To some it is a competition, to others it is not. All I know is that it sure hurts to lose. I remember being in Greensboro, North Carolina, between contracts. There was a dinner theatre holding auditions for a comedic play. I did some research and found out that the play had premiered at the Burt Reynolds Dinner Theatre, and that Charles Nelson Reilly had played the character for which I was auditioning. I thought, "Charles Nelson Reilly? I can do this, I've been trained by great professors, I've got this!"

I did not have that. Not getting the part crushed me. But actors cannot let failure get them down. I picked myself up and went to Fall Southeastern Theatre Conference in Atlanta that year and got back to work. Actors push through failure and persevere.

Sissy Spacek (2012) said, "All the times I felt like I was spinning my wheels trying to get ahead in New York, and all the times I would call home tired and discouraged, my mother would say to me, 'Sissy, as soon as you meet someone who's smart enough to realize how talented you are, you'll be on your way.' Bill Treusch turned out to be the person she was talking about" (120). She was a singer when she met Bill, but he encouraged her to try acting. No matter how hard it gets, no matter how many times the answer is no, if someone wants to be an actor, they have got to keep going. If you believe in yourself, you will find the strength to keep working until the answer is "yes."

In every age there are actors who work because they have no choice. To not act would drive them insane. When I was in high school, a guidance counselor asked me, in order to figure out a career path, "What would you do if you had a million dollars? Whatever it is, that's the kind of job you need to get."

I answered, "Somebody will pay me to sit at home and watch TV?" Close. It turns out I would rather be making the show than watching it, and I prefer live theatre to an electronic box.

Actors act because they love acting. As Rita Moreno (2013) said, she discovered that from an early age, performing made her deliriously happy. "I could escape any worries and past grief when I performed. I felt I was free, flying, above everyday concerns (and I still do feel that way when I perform). Work that you love is the purist escape; it is also salvation" (63).

With that in mind, next class I will be offering that which Moreno describes by offering you the chance to perform.

Homework

Students should prepare the final stages of their Monologue #2 rehearsal. The class after next class is monologue rehearsal. Students are required to be completely off-book, with blocking, gestures, and business. Each student actor will be watched by the rest of the class, who will be allowed to offer feedback.

- Students should bring writing utensils for the taking of notes. If you use electronic devices for note taking, make sure they are fully charged and mute them during class.
- Students should treat this as a dress rehearsal.
- Student performers will get professor feedback for how to specifically improve their performances so that they can maximize their positive grading potential.

Lesson 12
Stage Fright—Boo!

Exercise 1
1. Class should break into student groups. In each separate group, members should discuss the concept of stage fright: define it, describe it, etc.
2. Each group will subsequently share their answers and thoughts with the rest of the class.
3. Based on all discussions, the class as one group will come to a consensus as to the nature of stage fright.
4. Students are encouraged to share examples and stories of stage fright episodes they have experienced, witnessed, or heard about.

Stage fright is not actually fear of the stage—no actor with stage fright walks out, looks down, and screams, "Oh no, I'm standing on a stage!" and then runs for the wings while attempting to not touch the stage with their feet as they escape. Stage fright is the fear of performing in front of an audience of other people. Since the actor exists to perform for an audience, one can see why this debilitating fear can be quite the serious problem. It is an existential threat for the actor and a terrible thing.

Alan Cumming (2014) shared his thoughts about stage fright in relation to singing. The idea of singing could "send me into paroxysms of panic and even with major rehearsal could induce severe, almost insurmountable nerves . . . I'm not normally like that about acting. I'm usually quite relaxed about that, except for opening nights. And of course the more you do something, the more comfortable you become, and the less frightening it becomes" (228). Let us unpack that quote. He says he usually does not experience stage fright for acting except for on opening nights. This leads to the conclusion that one cause of stage fright is a lack of exposure to performing the piece in question in front of people. He also concludes that the more you do it, the less stage fright you have. This can mean that one cure for stage fright is to become overly familiar with the material through extensive rehearsals.

The Addams Family

Panic and severe nerves are symptoms. Some people suffer from chronic anxiety and panic attacks. If you do not and wonder what it is like, imagine experiencing stage fright, that fear you have right before you perform, only it lasts all day. Human beings fear the unknown, and that is a major component of what makes actors experience stage fright. Actors do not know how the material will be received or how the audience will react to their performance, and since people cannot know the future, actors have no idea how the performance will go. A big part of the fear is terror at the idea of screwing up in front of witnesses. If actors mess up in rehearsal and nobody is there, there is no one to sneer and laugh at them. If actors mess up in front of other people, actors cannot deny it happened and they cannot rationalize it away. There are witnesses, and their recollection shapes reality as much as does that of the actors.

It is in reaction to these witnesses that stage fright is born. The witnesses to the actor's performance become a threat, and so, just as when a person is faced with any sort of threat, the actor feels fear. Stage fright is a defense mechanism, a fight-or-flight reaction that silently yells at the person's body to "Run! Run you fool! Run!"

People have a residual self-image, like Neo in the first *Matrix* movie when Morpheus takes him up to the roof in the training program prior to the leap test. Morpheus points out that Neo's hair, clothes, and body have all changed from how they look outside the computer programs, and that this is how Neo sees himself.

An actor's residual self-image is presumably someone who is talented, competent, able, worth watching, and all in all a good and noble creature. If the actor screws up in front of the audience, makes foolish mistakes, and ultimately fails when they should succeed at acting, the audience's perception of the actor will erase their self-image and replace it with the audience's conception of them. The audience's image of the actor, bolstered by the evidence of their botched performance, will erase and replace the actor's self-image, destroying them as surely as would a machete attack. In the audience's mind, the actor becomes a no-talent imbecile, a loser, and that perception to some extent becomes the actor's reality.

Stage fright, then, is at its core a fear of rejection. Amy Poehler writes about handling rejection despite fear, which is an ability actors need to learn. She writes that the initial episodes of her series, *Parks and Recreation,* were not well received. "We kept our heads down and did our jobs. We controlled the only thing we could, which was the show. We did the thing. Because remember, the talking about the thing isn't the thing. The doing of the thing is the thing" (Poehler 2014, 253). A great way for actors to combat stage fright is to focus not on themselves but on something outside of them.

As an actor, you are more likely to succumb to stage fright if the small percentage of your mind that monitors your performance is focused on:

- What do I sound like?
- What do I look like?
- What are they thinking right now?
- Do they like me?
- Do they hate me?
- Am I boring them?
- Am I any good?
- Do they think I am stupid?
- Do they think I am ugly?

These thoughts are a recipe for disaster. Focus instead on things outside yourself, like being the character in the moment honestly chasing your objective. If you pretend you do not know the outcome, as your character does not know if they will be victorious or not, you will have to devote your energy to the objective's pursuit.

Focus on making sure you are correctly executing your gestures, business, and blocking. Focus on your vocal apparatus and monitor your breathing. Make sure you are breathing correctly, speaking with proper support, enunciating clearly, and that you are properly aiming your projected voice.

Concentrate and sincerely visualize the other character that is your character's visual focus. Conjure them and fully imagine their reactions to what your character is saying and doing. Put copious amounts of energy and concentration on entirely imagining their performance, doubling your efforts because you are playing two characters at once, your character and the invisible other to whom your character reacts. If you are wholly involved in creating every aspect of a complete performance, there will be nothing left to get nervous or frightened about.

There are many causes of stage fright, perhaps as varied as the sea of humanity itself. Each person is a separate individual, and each person has a different form of stage fright unique to that individual. However, the most common cause of stage fright is a lack of preparation. People become afraid because they fear the unknown; in this case, the unknown is your monologue because you are not completely off-book, or you are under-rehearsed. You are afraid of what you do not know: the words and blocking of your own audition piece.

There is a short play by Christopher Durang entitled *The Actor's Nightmare*. In it, an actor finds himself onstage during a show. He does not know what play it is or what character he is playing, and despite this ignorance, the show goes on and he is required to keep up. It is called the actor's nightmare because the common fright that actors have is being onstage and not knowing what they are supposed to do next.

Any actor who has been in a performance has had a spot of memory lapse. Hopefully the line either came back or their acting partner saved them. If the actor is doing a monologue, there is no one to save the actor. I have been the actor who needed saving. I have also been the actor who saved others. It is a glorious sight when you are looking at an acting partner, and suddenly their eyes widen, they look at the floor, their mouth drops open, and then they look at you with perhaps the most pleading look in human history as they silently beg you to save them from the actor's nightmare into which they have been dumped.

Over-rehearsing is one way to control and overcome stage fright. There is no such thing as over-rehearsing. Over-rehearsing is just enough and allows the actor to perform with confidence. An actor who is confident onstage is a wonder to behold. And confidence, as Mindy Kaling (2015) says, comes from hard work. "People talk about confidence without ever bringing up hard work. That's a mistake. . . . I don't understand how you could have self-confidence if you don't do the work" (218). She goes on to say, "I'm usually hyper-prepared for whatever I set my mind to do, which makes me feel deserving of attention and professional success, when that's what I'm seeking" (218). How awesome is her attitude? She does not get stage fright because she has worked super hard to get ready for the performance, and because of that she deserves to be the center of attention and has earned the right to be rewarded.

Her philosophy is that confidence is not something that people inherently possess, it is something people earn. "It's just that the truth is, I have never, ever, ever met a highly confident and successful person who is not what a movie would call a 'workaholic.'" She concludes, "Because confidence is like respect; you have to earn it" (Kaling 2015, 220).

The Addams Family

As a beginning actor in an Acting I class, you may have scant performing experience, and the unknown quotient can be alarming. In order to combat first-time audience jitters, especially with Monologue #2, you may want to assemble a test audience and perform for them before you perform in class for a grade.

Theatre is not complete until the audience is present. If actors perform a play and no one is there to watch it, they have not performed the play, they have only rehearsed it. Theatre does not exist absent the audience; it is the necessary ingredient to complete the recipe. For actors in this class, rehearsing pieces during class time is designed to help, but these are still rehearsals and not performances. In performance, there is no starting over if the actor messes up. In performance, there is no calling for line. In performance, actors are trapeze artists performing without a net.

For the purposes of this class, if you can gather friends or family and create a performance environment, it can go a long way towards finalizing your preparation for performance day. You can come in for that test confident, invigorated, and excited. You can believe in yourself. Like Alan Cumming (2014) says when he ruminates about how his father would tell him he was awful and his mother would tell him he was wonderful, "I didn't fully believe what either of my parents said about me, and I've taken that approach in dealing with critics of my work. 'If you believe the good ones, you have to believe the bad ones' is my mantra. The most important opinion, of both my work and my conduct in life, is my own" (133). Actors believe in themselves, and as an actor, you can accomplish that through hard work.

Exercise 2

1. The class should break into groups.
2. Each group should discuss solutions to stage fright. What can someone do about it? Create answers and thoughts in each group. Share anecdotes.
3. Each group will share their answers, thoughts, and anecdotes with the rest of the class.
4. As a class, come to a consensus as to solutions and what can be done to assure perseverance in the face of terror.

Stage fright can be a good thing as long as the actor controls it rather than allowing it to control them. If you are an actor who has stage fright, that is actually a good thing because it means you care about your work and you care about other people's feelings. It means you value other people and care that they like your work. Stage fright means that acting is important to you, so having it is not necessarily a total disaster.

The Addams Family

Stage fright creates adrenalin, and that is something actors can use to improve their performance. As Betty White (2011) says, you have to work your way through it. "Let me be clear: *you are never calm*. But your job is to deliver." She goes on to say, "None of the tricks I try work," and that "It's amazingly common for actors to have some form of stage fright. It just manifests itself in different ways." She adds that when an actor tells you that she does not get stage fright, she is "lying through her teeth" (116). As to where it comes from, she also believes it is a fear of forgetting lines, a fear of blanking out, and a fear of making a fool of oneself (118).

Actors must be brave. Bravery is not the absence of fear; bravery is doing what needs to be done despite the fear. Students in this class must strive to be brave. Persevere. Screw fear!

Lesson 13
Monologue #2 Rehearsal
Tragic or Serious Monologue

The way for today to be a success is for student actors to treat this rehearsal as a performance. Student actors, when you are called to the performance space, do what you have rehearsed so far on your own in preparation for today. Once you are done, you will receive feedback and you will find out what worked and what needs improvement. The purpose of rehearsal is to improve your performance. It is not to encourage people to laud you with compliments and tell you how awesome you are. All actors, no matter how talented, can use an outside eye to evaluate their performance and give tips on how their work can improve.

In a way, being cast in a show is a compliment. There are many types of directors. Some directors may include lots of compliments in their notes. I know directors who give a negative note to an actor and follow that up with a positive note, a "This didn't work," followed by a "But this was wonderful." Some directors give what is called a compliment sandwich, where they tell the actor something nice, then something negative, then end with another compliment. To me, all that does is double and triple the amount of time it takes to give notes at the end of rehearsal when all actors want to do is go home. Besides, as an actor, no matter how many compliments I get, the only thing I remember after rehearsal is the weaknesses the director asked me to address. The director who gives me compliments is wasting time. It's nice, don't get me wrong—I love it when people give me compliments. In fact, if you want to tell me how awesome this book is, please do!

It feels nice to receive compliments from peers, but the goal is to improve the performance. Compliments might make an actor feel good about themselves, but what will make the actor feel better is making a great impression on their audience and a good grade on their monologue performance. The class will improve your performance through constructive criticism that will lead to you doing the best acting job and making the best grade possible on performance day.

Rehearsal Methodology

1. The actors need to do vocal and physical warm-ups.
2. Either through volunteering or drafting, actors will perform their monologues for the class in the following manner:
   - Opening slate
   - Piece
   - Closing slate
3. Opening slate is actor name, name of character to be played, name of play, playwright; closing slate is a bow and a form of "Thank you."
4. Performing actors may call for line if they have someone on-book.
5. Those not performing should watch their classmates perform and take notes. Strive to note ways in which the acting can be improved, or compliment things that deeply impressed you.
6. When the professor gives feedback to an actor, all class members should pay heed. The notes the professor gives to the actor on the boards may be applicable to all student actors. This is the most practical learning phase of the whole semester, when real acting happens and is analyzed as to how it can improve. This is not theory; this is practice. This is experience: where true learning occurs.
7. Actors receiving notes should write them down so that they do not forget the notes. In this manner, actors make progress. If an actor performs and makes a mistake, and the professor gives a note on that mistake, and the actor forgets the note and so never applies it to future performances, no progress will be made. Progress means that the actor receives a note from a professor, absorbs it, applies the lesson to the performance, and thereby improves it.

Grades

All art is subjective. Trust your professor to make an informed opinion about the performing arts and what it takes to be successful at acting. In the end, it is up to the audience how they react to an actor's performance. It is something actors can only control by orchestrating their performances in order to get specific reactions from an audience. But once an actor is emoting on stage, they have given control of artistic interpretation to the audience. That is also true of an audience of one, or in this case, the professor grading the class. The grading template is as objective a grading template as I can make, but an actor's best formula for success is to take the notes they are given in the next two class days of rehearsal and incorporate the notes into their performance, so that in the professor audience's opinion, the performance is the best it can be.

Now on to rehearsal. Who wants to be first?

Lesson 14
Day Two
Monologue #2 Rehearsal
Tragic or Serious Monologue

1. Class members will perform vocal and physical warm-ups
2. Acting students will rehearse monologues.
3. Acting students will receive feedback.

Acting I Monologue #2 Evaluation

Student _____ Time _____

Grade Awarded _____

I. Physical performance
   A. Body language: did movements support/illustrate the words spoken?
   B. Control: was there erroneous movement?
   C. Visual focus: did the actor appear to be talking to a finite point/person?
   D. Facial expressions: did they support/illustrate the words spoken?
II. Vocal performance
   A. Pace
   B. Volume
   C. Pitch
   D. Quality
III. Characterization
   A. Need: was desire obvious?
   B. Objective: did the character appear to have a tangible goal?
   C. Action: was it organized and directed towards objective?
   D. Transformation: was the character emotionally committed?
IV. Mechanics
   A. Memorization
   B. Commitment
V. Overall performance

Lesson 15
Performance Day Monologue #2
Tragic or Serious Monologue

1. Actors will perform vocal and physical warm-ups
2. Class members will take notes on each performance.
   A. If there is no time to react to all performances in this class period, please bring these notes to the next class so that all performers can receive reactions.
   B. The class will hear everyone's notes aloud.
   C. Strive to identify two strengths and two weaknesses for each performer.
3. Actors, take the space when called. Do not begin until the professor signals you to begin.
4. After each performance, the professor will finish making notes. The next performer can take the space, but do not begin until the professor has finished evaluating the previous performer and is ready to evaluate you.
5. The professor will take the notes made today and after class use them to formulate student actor grades. Students will receive written evaluations during the next class.
6. Once everyone has performed, the class will create the Circle of Feedback.
   A. In the Circle of Feedback, the class will arrange the furniture into a circle.
   B. The professor will lead the class in discussion by going around the circle and eliciting comments about each monologue performance in the order in which they were performed.
   C. First round of the circle is to discuss strengths or anything the class members believe the actor did well.
   D. Second round of the circle is to discuss weaknesses, or ways class members believe the actor could improve.

E. Any conflicting or confusing notes should be discussed by the actor with the professor either after class or during office hours if not addressed during circle time.

Homework

Next class, student actors should bring a comedic or funny monologue. Students should repeat the procedure followed for the tragic or serious monologue, only this time with a speech from a play categorized as a comedy.

Lesson 16
Hard Work
If You Can Get It

The Director, hard at work.

Exercise 1
Student actors should present the written copy of their comedy monologue to the professor.

There is a play titled *Nice Work If You Can Get It*, with music and lyrics by George and Ira Gershwin and book by Joe DiPietro. The play is about bootlegging liquor in 1927, but the title is more a reference to falling in love. It is nice to fall in love, and if someone wants to be an actor, especially in the theatre, it is vital that they love acting. Acting in the theatre is nice work, but it is hard work, grueling, in fact. If someone is contemplating any other way to live life, when things get hard in the theatre, and things will, that someone will be severely tempted to abandon the stage unless they are absolutely devoted to it.

Out of all the different kinds of acting, acting in plays, be they musical or straight, is the hardest kind of acting one can do. Congratulations, students in this class, on having the courage and the daring to be the hardest-working and the best! Terrence Mann, in a video titled *Auditions and Insights with Terrence Mann,* teaches a class to a group of high school students at a theatre conference. He tells them that if they want to be famous, they should do movies. If they want to be rich, they should do television. If they want to be good, they should do theatre. In his opinion and the opinions of other artists who have worked in various media, theatre is the most difficult.

Alec Baldwin (2017) wrote, "The most fulfilling experiences I've had as an actor have been in the theater, the only medium I could count on for a reliably satisfying artistic result. It was the only place I could bring what I had to offer and believe that it mattered. . . . More important, it is where you have the chance to grow in some meaningful way" (250). So, some double good news. The first bit of good news is that while it is hard, stage acting is very rewarding. It makes you feel good about yourself; your artistic contribution has more significance and you learn something because it challenges you and forces you to grow.

Of Mice and Men

The second piece of good news is that acting for the stage is only hard if you are doing it right. In response to the question of what advice she would give to young actors, Betty White (2011) said that they should "Treat your profession with respect," and to "Come in prepared." She advised, "Walk in to every situation with a positive, open mind. Allow yourself time to experience a situation before forming an opinion." She also advised young actors to be grateful, avoid bad behavior, and "If you're not enthusiastic, just lie down and close your eyes and be *very* quiet" (254).

Coming in prepared means doing all the work before actor call time. Laziness kills good acting. An actor who does not respect the work disrespects their fellow actors, their director, the performing arts, and ultimately the audience. The audience often buys their tickets, but even if admission is free, the audience is taking the time and effort to come and watch a work of culture that theatre artists have proposed is vital to living a quality life. To tell audiences that art improves their lives and is an essential component of a worthy civilization and to then not do the work would be a betrayal of the audience present in the theatre and all of humanity.

What Betty White could mean when she advises young actors who lack enthusiasm to be quiet and lie down is for them to vamoose. Lie down so the other actors can use unenthusiastic actors as rugs to walk across. They can be quiet, so the devoted actors do not have to listen to their pointless drivel. If an actor is apathetic and lacks enthusiasm, that actor should not be in the play. That actor has taken a spot that could be occupied by someone dedicated and happy to be acting even if it is hard work. Unenthusiastic actors should go away, Betty White seems to be saying—a viewpoint worth discussion.

Some people, when faced with a hard work challenge, will rise to the occasion. They will clear their lives of distraction; they will focus their energies and attention on the work at hand. They will exert mighty efforts to accomplish their objectives with integrity and honor. Those are good actors, regardless of talent level. Then there are the other kind of actors, who, when faced with a hard work challenge, will not rise to the challenge.

If someone gets through a monologue or scene but doesn't do all the work, all they get is a grade. Students are in school to gain knowledge and education, not grades. The grade is supposed to represent what the student has learned, not that the student has learned nothing. They have paid the school for a product or service and then stolen it from themselves by not doing the work. They did not cheat the school or the professor. They cheated themselves out of that for which they paid the school. A test is as much to measure if the class is teaching students as it is to measure if the students are learning. If students don't do the work, they are denying themselves the opportunity to learn, which is why they are even in school.

Imagine that someone makes their way through school and graduates with a degree. The degree is meant to symbolize their possession of specialized knowledge and skills. Because they have the degree, a business hires them. Because they only survived college and learned none of the knowledge and skills the job requires, they are unable to do the job, and so the company fires them. Therefore, not doing all the work in class is a bad idea.

The work some students might skip includes not doing the research, not doing the script analysis, barely memorizing the lines, not blocking movement or planning business, under-rehearsing, and generally depending on talent and luck to get through a performance assignment. These are all things that, should a student indulge in them, will make that student an actor who lacks integrity. In addition to being honest and having good morals and ethics, integrity also means, according to Dictionary.com, "the stage of being whole, entire or undiminished." Only an actor who works with integrity can achieve great work. There are no shortcuts for greatness. Acting is not about getting by with the least amount of effort. Not doing the work is a betrayal of self and denies students the chance of reaching their full potential. Students should stay true to themselves. Of integrity, Sissy Spacek (2012) says, "Nothing I accomplished would be worth salt if I lost track of who I really was" (111).

Actors, just like real people, grow old. As they get older, they will amass more and more memories. Also, as people age, their tendency to examine and relive their memories grows more prevalent. Eventually, they become senior citizens, perhaps in a rocking chair, reliving memories as they consume Jell-O because not only is it tasty, but it is good for their joints. People want to have good memories. The way to have good memories in the future is to live life well in the present. People can avoid the doom of sitting in that future chair filled with regrets such as "I could have been a great actor, if only I had done the work. If I could go back, I would do the work." Students should do the work now so that they can be proud of themselves for the rest of their lives.

Doing the work, even when it is hard, is more fun, and that begins in school, yea, even unto this class. Do you want to regret your monologue performances in your old age, or do you want to look back at this time of your life and say, "I nailed that comedic monologue in Acting I!" or "I was so great in that scene we did!"

Part of doing great in class is attending class on a regular basis. Student attendance in class is mandatory and students only get a small number of absences before the college drops them from the class. Students' actual physical presence in the classroom is considered part of the workload, so if students do not come to class, they are not doing a significant amount of the class work.

124 Acting: Year One

Of Mice and Men

Every day in class, and not just in lectures, acting theory will be discussed. If students are not in class, they will not receive this information; therefore, they will be unable to apply these ideas to their performances. The performance evaluations in acting class are based on how well students apply the ideas and practices discussed in class to their performances. If a student is not in class, never hears the ideas, and never applies them to the performance, that student's performance evaluation will suffer because they did not apply the discussed theories and techniques.

On rehearsal days, while other actors are rehearsing, class attendance remains a vital ingredient in the learning process. Watching other actors shows two things: what the other actors do that does not work, and what the other actors do that is successful. In addition, notes given to other actors on their rehearsal are not useless to other actors; rather those notes are relevant to all actors. Chances are, any note a professor gives after a rehearsal to one actor is relevant to their classmates. While the note may be for another actor, students should assess whether it is applicable to what they are doing, and if so, apply those lessons to their performances.

For instance, an actor rehearsing their scene looks down at the floor too much, or up at the ceiling too much, or tends to walk sideways rather than looking where they are going. The actor gets notes from the professor telling them why looking at the floor or ceiling is a weak choice unless it is an action motivated by the script, because it is usually indicates a nervous actor looking for their lines. Or that cheating out looks unnatural when walking; it is the actor trying to stay fully open to the audience and it creates awkward physicality for the character. After the professor gives that actor those notes, if the next actor gets up and does the exact same thing because they were not listening to the previous notes, they missed a learning opportunity. It is an inefficient use of rehearsal time. Everyone can learn from everyone else.

What if, for some reason, a student does not like going to class? Unfortunately, not everything in life can be pleasant, and not everything in life is fun. Carrie Fisher, in addition to being an actor, was also an alcoholic and addict. As such, it was a really good idea for her to attend Alcoholics Anonymous or Narcotics Anonymous meetings. She once said of going to meetings:

> *I heard someone say that I didn't have to like the meetings, I just had to go to them. Well this was a revelation to me! I thought I had to like everything I did.... But if what this person told me were true, then I didn't actually have to be comfortable all the time. If I could, in fact, learn to experience a quota of discomfort, it would be awesome news. And if I could consistently go to that three-hour meeting, I could also exercise, and I could write. In short, I could actually be responsible. (Fisher 2008, 106)*

Of Mice and Men

Being responsible, what a concept. People do not brush their teeth because it is fun; they brush their teeth because it is necessary work. For an acting student, attending class and performing all the preparatory steps are work that needs to be done.

Students in school need to do the work. As an undergraduate, there were times when I fell prey to the belief that if I was in a show, it was okay to skip class or let my coursework slide because the show was more important. In the pyramid of priorities, because the reputation of the school rests on the quality of its productions, there may appear to be some truth to the belief that the show is more important than the class, but this is not so. The true reputation of the school comes from the quality of the graduates it produces, and quality graduates are created in the classroom.

Actors do not shirk classroom duties simply because of a show. It is not a proper balancing of priorities. Students are better served if they properly manage their time and resources so that they can be simultaneously a success in production and in academics.

The purpose of schoolwork is to prepare the student for success in the real job world, so if a student cannot handle the workload in school, what else can be concluded that they will be unable to handle the real job workload? If students cannot do their homework in school, they will not be able to do their homework at a job. If students cannot follow directions in the classroom, they will be unable to follow a supervisor's instructions at a real job, causing the supervisor to consider terminating the former student's employment.

If one has no interest in academia, one might wonder as to why one has chosen to go to college. Less than 1 percent of the world's population even has the opportunity to attend college, so it is a wonderful idea for the students in this class to be in school. They have chosen to go to college. Once here, students can choose to be positive, open-minded, and enthusiastic. They can choose to learn as much as possible and grow; or they can choose to be miserable and negative. Negativity makes learning difficult, but the choice to be positive or negative is up to the individual student.

Acting for the stage and studying acting as a college student both take true dedication. Judi Dench (2010) says, "To those who are just starting out on their careers, I advise them not to do it at all if there is anything else they want to do. I also advise them that they mustn't do it if they haven't got great reserves of energy, because there is no point if you are a tired person" (238). If an actor has other interests, hobbies that will distract them and take up their time, they may choose to pursue those activities when they should be rehearsing, resting, or sleeping. Some acting professors start their classes with the admonishment that the students should be prepared to "Eat, breathe, and excrete" acting for the rest of the semester or drop the class immediately. Their point is that being a good actor takes dedication.

Robert DeNiro serves as an example of the commitment necessary for success. In discussing his transformation for *Raging Bull*, he said, "I just can't fake acting. I know movies are an illusion, and maybe the first rule is to fake it, but not for me. I'm too curious. I want the experience. I want to deal with all the facts of the character, thin or fat" (Levy 2014, 240). If someone does something halfway, or fakes it, they will never achieve the level of quality that will make them truly happy and proud of their work. Acting reflects identity. People create their own societal identities, their social roles. Someone can be a great actor who commits to the work and fully accomplishes artistic goals and feels a sense of pride, or they can be a mediocre actor who does the bare minimum, only goes through the motions, and is never truly proud of their work. People choose who they become.

One hard thing about acting is that actors never get any time off when they are preparing for a play's run. I have a joke I tell students that goes like this: "You know the great thing about being a director? You want to watch me work on the play?" I close my eyes for a few seconds and think. Then I open my eyes and say, "See? That was me working on the play!" The flip side of that, for actors as well as directors, is that artists are always thinking about their performance; they are always working.

West Side Story

Jack Nicholson discussed the need to work hard when he said, "To succeed—in order to become a Brando or a Bob Dylan, you can't just punch a time card, take a nap, and pick up your reviews and your money . . . your work is all-consuming . . . whether you want to or not you do take your work home with you" (Eliot 2013, 142). Actors are always working when they are in show mode. Here is another thing that is hard: to some extent, an actor is their own boss.

Especially in the preparation stage, acting can be a lonely profession. Research, analysis, preparation, memorization, solo rehearsal time—these are usually self-motivated, solitary activities. Actors do not have someone following them around saying, "You should do some script analysis work this hour," or "You should be rehearsing and fine-tuning blocking now," or "Time to study lines!" Actors must decide for themselves when it is time to work, how long to work, and when the work is done, which, recall, is not until the performance event is completely over.

While the job of acting entails lying to everyone else, actors must never lie to themselves. The actor must be self-aware and artistically disciplined. An actor cannot lie to themselves by saying things like, "This is fine, I don't need to research this," or "I stumbled on a couple of words, but I've got this; it will work itself out in performance." It will not. Small problems become grossly magnified under the microscope of public performance.

Actors need to know their strengths and weaknesses. Knowing their strengths is good because this will help them to keep from shoring up a weak performance by hiding behind their strengths, which leads actors to develop a catalog of tricks or gimmicks that they depend on from show to show rather than giving honest, individualized portrayals for each character. All actors fall prey to this habit at some time, even greats like Tom Hanks. I have studied his work extensively, and even in the advent of his greatest achievement, *Forrest Gump,* there are two moments in which I saw old Tom Hanks tricks rather than genuine Forrest Gump moments. Granted, that is only two moments, and he's on screen for almost the entire two hours and twenty-two minutes of that film. He very much deserved the Oscar that he was awarded for the work. I want to be Tom Hanks.

An actor who knows their strengths avoids wasting rehearsal time and resources working on things that they are good at; instead, they can focus on getting strong in their weak spots. This self-knowledge is important because an actor's set of strengths and weaknesses will fluctuate throughout life. Ignored, strengths become weaknesses. Work on weaknesses makes them strong. The strength-weakness continuum is like a great ocean in a constant state of fluctuating movement, shifting from one side to the next.

Self-awareness is good because actors need to know their value as a product. Acting, and by extension theatre, is art, but in the professional world it is a business, and the product actors are pitching for consumption is themselves. When actors audition, they want the casting director to hire them and pay them money. When actors are in a show, they want the audience to buy tickets. Actors need to know what they have to offer, what benefits they bring to the table, how they can make the show and the company better, how they can make the audience members' lives better because they watched the actors. This must stem from an honest assessment of the actors' abilities.

If everyone tells an actor that their singing is weak, the actor cannot tell themselves, "Oh, they just don't get it," and continue merrily along without doing anything to improve their singing. If everyone tells an actor that they do not move well, they cannot tell themselves, "That's only their opinion, I move great." That actor needs to do something to improve their movement. Feedback is vital so that actors can find out what areas need the most work and what they need to do in order to get better.

Sidney Poitier (2000) says, "I feel most critical of myself when I notice any trace of slovenliness in my work. My work is *me*, and I try my damnedest to take very good care of me, because I'm taking care of more than just the me that one sees. I'm taking care of the me that represents a hell of a lot more than me" (161). By "slovenly" he does not mean literally tattered or dirty; he means doing careless or slipshod work. Actors need to take care, be proud, represent all that they stand for with pride. Be assured without being smug or cocky. Be humble without being self-hating. A superior inferiority complex allows an actor to walk into rehearsal thinking that they are the best actor there while realizing that they also suck. This enables an actor to feel good about themselves without ignoring the areas in which they need to improve.

One strategy for actor improvement involves the actor identifying actors they think are good, finding out what their methodologies are, and emulating them. Sidney Poitier grew up as a young black man in the South of the United States during the Jim Crow era. This experience made him decide he was better than the people who declared him worthless:

> *Later, I would carry that theme, detached from questions of color and race, all the way into the theater world, where it would become a personal standard, applicable to creative excellence and professional competitiveness. Marlon Brando was an idol of mine, a consummate artist and one of the good guys. I aimed to be better than even him.* (Poitier 2000, 42)

Student actors can pick an actor they admire, study that actor's performances, do some research, and figure out how that actor manages to achieve their accomplishments, then strive to out-do the actor they admire.

Believe that you can be the best. Hard work earns success and recognition. This has nothing to do with talent, nothing to do with looks, nothing to do with how many people in the audience like you. This is about the work. If actors do the work well, their belief that they deserve success and recognition will be earned and it will prevent them from coming off to others as spoiled, entitled, and invidious.

The danger of talent is that it can make someone who depends on it lazy. Every time someone with talent relies on it to save them from hard work, they are taking a chance. Eventually their luck will run out, a performance will be subpar or perhaps even disastrous, and those artists will have failed humanity. Actors need to take the work seriously and take their responsibilities to humanity solemnly and zealously. Sissy Spacek (2012) says, "Sometimes we asked our parents big questions, such as 'How big is the universe?' and 'Why are we here?' Mother had the best answer to that one. 'You're here,' she said, 'to make the world a better place because you've lived'" (47). This philosophical responsibility is even more poignant for actors. Actors stand in front of their community and say, "Watch and listen to us and we will make your lives better. Pay us to pretend and we will show you the way." This responsibility for the health of humanity and the well-being of the collective soul is the reason why it is incumbent upon all actors to work hard, work smart, and work true.

At the same time, do not overwork. Actors need to find a balance between life and work. There is a level of having gone too far. Rehearse and work the lines enough, though, so that the words do not require thought. The words go from short-term memory and become firmly lodged in long-term memory. For example, there was a monologue that I performed for the first time when I was twenty-two years old. As of this writing I am fifty-eight years old. I still know that monologue. I am not saying actors need to remember lines for decades—so many, many decades—but the words need to be durably locked in long-term memory.

West Side Story

Once the words are locked, actors can commit themselves to the character's mental and emotional journey. The actor will be thinking the character's thoughts instead of wondering what words they are going to say next. The actor will be feeling the emotions those thoughts generate in the character rather than showing audiences how they feel about how their performance of the words is going. It will be as if their character thinks a thought, the audience sees on the actor's face and body how their character feels about that thought, then they think another thought and the audience sees how the character feels about that, and that string of thoughts, emotions, actions, and words becomes an indelible and ecstatic performance. Knowing the material well enough means that the actor can commit to the character's journey and not focus on the act of remembering, reciting, and recreating the words and blocking.

That is the target level of preparatory work student actors in this class need to do. There is no need to go beyond that. Judi Dench (2010) spoke of working on a play with her husband Michael and the temptation to continue to work even when the workday was done. "It was an enormous help that Michael was playing my husband, although we never talked about the theatre or work when we came home; perhaps a little bit in the car, but very little even then. I don't like to talk about a part outside rehearsal whilst I am still working on it. It takes the edge off the spontaneity for me" (93–94). Actors need not work on a piece so much that they kill the piece.

Actors can have a life outside of acting, so long as that life does not get in the way of their work; however, actors should not let work stop them from living. Actors can watch movies, surf the web, and socialize; they can surely do all of that, if they have done the day's work first. Do the work, then live. In the above example, Dame Judi was working with a professional company and had rehearsed about ten hours a day, so she had earned the right to leave the work when she went home.

In an Acting I class, once student actors have a performance assignment, be it a monologue or scene, they should devote an hour a day to it until the performance deadline has passed, the event is over and struck, and the students have moved on to their next assignment. If actors reach a point where all life seems to have been drained from the piece, they may have over-rehearsed. In that case, take a day or so off and then come back with renewed vigor. Keeping repeat performances fresh is the subject of Lesson 23.

Once the actor knows the piece, has rehearsed it often and well, and is sufficiently prepared, a major challenge is retaining the illusion of the first time in every performance. In this class students only perform each piece for a grade once. The challenge for students is to make sure that their performance reaches its peak of ripeness on performance day. Be not unripe or too green; prepare abundantly. But do not peak too soon and be rotten on the vine come show time. All the same, 'tis better to be over-ripe and work hard on the illusion of the first time, than to be green and too soon plucked from the vine and taken to market.

Exercise 1

1. The class should divide into four teams.
2. Each team should discuss amongst themselves the thing that their team believes represents the greatest challenge to an actor. In other words, what is the hardest thing about acting? Each group should come up with more than one in case another group has the same response.
3. The professor will poll groups to eliminate doubling of opinions so that each group has a different aspect of acting that they believe is the hardest thing about acting.
4. Each team develops a persuasive speech that explains and defends their position, making the case that of the four aspects of acting, theirs is the hardest.
5. Each team will present their argument. As they do, other teams will take notes and develop a counterargument as to why the other team is wrong in this manner:
   - Team 1 listens to Team 2.
   - Team 2 listens to Team 1.
   - Team 1 will attack and disprove Team 2.
   - Team 2 will attack and disprove Team 1.
   - Team 3 will listen to Team 4.
   - Team 4 will listen to Team 3.
   - Team 3 will attack and disprove Team 4.
   - Team 4 will attack and disprove Team 3.
6. After each team has been heard and all teams have had a chance to develop counterarguments, each team will take turns delivering their counterarguments. As this happens, the team being attacked will make notes on the counter argument and develop a refutation defense.
7. Once all teams have had a chance to develop their refutation defense, these defenses will be heard.

This entire process is an example of one of the hardest things for an actor to do: to make the character's pursuit of the superobjective vital and true. It is difficult to illustrate the intensity of the character's pursuit of the superobjective, and the minor objectives in each scene that lead to the superobjective. This transforms each line of dialogue into an action instead of simple talking. This shows the action the character is taking by how they deliver the line and how each subsequent line refines an argument like a debate. The actor delivers the lines with artistic and performative density, like poetry even when the work is prose, in that everything the actor says and does symbolizes something, stands for something, means something, and is active action distilled to its most potent state in a struggle that has life and death consequences.

Homework

1. Students should keep their Monologue #2, the serious monologue, fresh in their minds. The class will be using them in an exercise next class.
2. Students should bring a printed copy of Monologue #3, the comedic monologue, to the next class. The class will be using them in an exercise.

Lesson 17
The Difference Between Tragic and Comedic Acting

Is there a difference between acting in a serious play versus acting in a comedy? To find out, I did what any responsible researcher would do: I posted a question on Facebook. I asked, "What is the difference between acting in a serious play versus acting in a comedy?" Here are the answers I received:

1. "The actor."
2. "Timing . . . actor's timing and delivery, of course."
3. "A banana peel."
4. "Is there a difference? Play the truth either way."
5. "Many more pauses for laughter in one of them."
6. "There's a difference?"
7. "I remember you saying it's not that hard to make an audience laugh, but to make them gasp . . . that's difficult."
8. "I always think about not 'making the audience' do anything but "allowing the audience" to do whatever through truthful characterization."
9. "The energy put into keeping a straight face."
10. "According to Michael Green, the comic actor cast as a pirate needs to ask the director, 'Which shoulder should I sew my parrot upon?' The serious actor already knows."
11. "The script!"
12. "Nothing, just read the damn script."
13. "Comedy is more difficult."
14. "For me, comedies involve two different approaches. There are comedies that are very performance-based and in which the actors on stage play much bigger than life and interact with the audience in a more direct way. The fourth wall can kind of disappear at times in those works and they are just loads of fun! Then there are

more subtle comedies that require the actors to center themselves in more realistic portrayals. In the second type, I believe the approach an actor takes is essentially the same as he or she would adopt in a dramatic portrayal."
15. "It's easier to make people cry than to make 'em laugh."
16. "Timing!"
17. "For the writer, the sadness is in the spaces between the words in a comedy. The actor's body in a comedy inhabits those spaces."
18. "There is no difference. Follow the text and listen to your director."

To summarize these answers: there is no difference; the difference is in the timing; the only difference is the script; the difference is the presence of physical comedy in comedic acting; the technical needs of comedy are different, i.e., holding for laughs and not breaking character to laugh yourself; the actor is the only difference, with the actor of serious plays being more knowledgeable about theatre, however, at the same time the difference is that comedy is harder than serious plays. Number 17 seems to mean that the actor plays comedy with their mouth while portraying tragedy with their body, while Number 14 touches on style, which is what this chapter is about.

I have encountered theatre professionals who are of the opinion that all acting in serious plays needs to be in the style of realism, while all comedies need to be acted in a non-realistic style. The actor's job is the same regardless of the play's genre, but the way the actor accomplishes their job may change, and that is where acting styles enter the fray.

The Greeks believed there was a difference between acting in a serious play, or tragedy, and acting in a comedy. In my study of acting history, I have come to the following conclusions about Ancient Greek, Shakespearean, and classical acting theory regarding comedy versus tragedy. The Greeks had rules for the writing of plays. Only people of the noble class could be lead characters in a serious play, whereas average citizens were the subjects of their comedies. Tragedies had to be written in poetry, whereas comedies required prose. One of the purposes of Greek tragedy was to ennoble the audience; by watching their society's best people act heroically even at the worst of times, the audience would strive to be better people. Conversely, comedies focused on the basest aspects of human existence, like sex jokes, bathroom humor, and slapstick physicality to draw amusement from humanity's debasement. Such disparate goals require a difference in methodology. The same methods cannot be used to both glorify humanity and to degrade people. Actors move and speak one way to show the nobility of spirit and another way to show the grossness of the physical body.

This harkens to the differences between opera and musical comedy. Opera was an attempt by Italian artists in the eighteenth century to recre-

King Lear

ate what they believed Greek tragedy was like. Compare an opera with a contemporary musical comedy and you create a picture of the differences between acting in a classical serious play and acting in a comedy. Opera has vast, ornate, and splendid sets, costumes, lighting, and sound design. Musical comedies are usually meant to symbolize a contemporary environment through the elements of set design. The singing style and the bearing of the characters in an opera are dark, serious, and musically opulent. The mien of characters in a musical comedy tends to be bright, positive, with music much more popular and contemporary in nature. The performance tactics of an opera singer are exceedingly different from those of a musical comedy performer.

    The singing style of an opera star coupled with the movement style of opera choreography, when compared to the singing style and choreography of a musical comedy celebrant, marks the different approaches to the creation and enacting of these individuated yet similar performance arts. The singing style of the opera artist is similar to the vocal style of an actor in a serious play, whereas the singing style of the musical comedy artist is akin to the vocal characteristics of an actor in a comedy.

    The dance style in an opera versus a musical comedy is comparable to an actor's physicality when performing a role in a serious play versus a comedy. If one looks at dance—which, like acting, is a performance art—one can see the impact style has on a performer's technique. For instance, tap and ballet are both forms of dance, but they are very different from each other. Tap is not ballet, ballet is not tap, and yet they are both dancing. The ballet dancer and the tap dancer can perform the same choreography, but because their form and disposition are so dissimilar, the performances may bear an infinitesimal resemblance to each other. The steps are the same but the way they are composed is different. This distinction is style.

There is style in acting as there is in dancing and singing. In the Theatre Appreciation class at Pensacola State College, we use Edwin Wilson's text, *The Theatre Experience.* In the section on theatrical genres, Wilson briefly examines the different forms of comedy in theatre, identifying the six major forms of comedy as farce, burlesque, satire, domestic comedy, comedy of manners, and comedy of ideas. In Wilson's definitions of these theatrical comedic forms, most of his descriptions detail a physical style that involves different levels of exaggeration.

The definitions are as follows, with the underlines for emphasis from me. For farce: "Farce thrives on <u>exaggeration</u>—not only plot complications but also <u>broad physical humor</u> and stereotyped characters. . . . Mock violence, rapid movement, and accelerating pace are hallmarks of farce" (Wilson 2015, 184).

For burlesque, Wilson writes, "Burlesque also relies on <u>knockabout physical humor</u>, as well as <u>gross exaggerations</u> and, occasionally, vulgarity" (Wilson 2015, 184).

For satire: "Satire uses wit, irony and <u>exaggeration</u> to attack or expose evil and foolishness" (Wilson 2015, 184).

The definitions of domestic comedy, comedy of manners, and comedy of ideas have no references to physical humor or exaggerations of any kind. These are relatively realistic forms of comedy. The other three forms—farce, burlesque, and satire—are more non-realistic forms of comedy.

The non-realistic forms of comedy depend on exaggeration; the physical rules that govern the lives and behaviors of the characters are different from those in serious, realistic plays. One of the reasons the physicality in comedies tends to be different from realistic, serious plays is because the purposes of comedy and tragedy are different.

The tragic or serious character is meant to be representative of the audience member. The audience is meant to empathize with and project themselves into the character so that the drama is happening to the audience member. The audience becomes the vicarious hero. The audience cares deeply for the character and goes on the journey with the character; the audience feels that what happens to the character is happening to them.

Comedy does not create empathy between the character and the audience. We are not meant to care what happens to the lead character, because if we care what happens, we will not laugh. The audience will be too worried that the character was physically harmed and will not find anything funny. People may find it funny when a stranger trips and falls because they do not know them and are not emotionally invested in their well-being. It is not funny when someone they love, like a beloved and elderly Meemaw, trips and falls.

King Lear

In early 1990, I was walking across the quad at Lindenwood University and heard that commercial for Life Alert in which the old lady looks at the camera and tremulously declares, "I've fallen, and I can't get up!" A couple of students had snatched her line, put it on a tape loop, and then put their extremely loud stereo speakers in their dorm window and were playing the line over and over. You could hear the two students laughing after each take. They literally sounded like Beavis and Butt-Head laughing. You would hear, "I've fallen, and I can't get up," then the two of them laughing, then a repeat of the line, then more laughing, and this went on for as long as I was in earshot. It is funny when a stranger on TV falls, but in life, if beloved Meemaw falls, people do not laugh. Rather, they yell, "Oh no! Grandma's fallen! She's bleeding! Someone help my Meemaw! Call 911!"

Because of the audience's need to empathize with the serious or tragic hero, often serious plays are done in the style of realism. Because audiences need to understand that no matter what happens, the comedic protagonist is going to be okay, and so that audiences will accept slapstick comedy, comedic plays are often produced in a non-realistic style.

Lesson 17—The Difference Between Tragic and Comedic Acting

Both tragedy and comedy plays are meant to improve society. While that goal is the same, the approach is different. Tragedy and its descendant, the serious play, seek to teach lessons about the individual. The tragic play focuses on life lessons the audience can learn by placing themselves in the protagonist's shoes. By learning from the example of the protagonist's story, individuals will each live life better. People will not make the same choices the lead characters made. The message is "Do not be like Oedipus: do not kill your father and marry your mother, because patricide and incest are bad. Do not be like Medea: be nice and civil in your divorce proceedings and do not kill your children. Do not be like Macbeth: do not kill the king. Do not be like Hamlet: if the ghost of your father appears to you and demands vengeance, call a priest and have the spirit cleansed from the house. Do not be like Willy Loman: do not cheat on your wife, and do not get caught in a sleazy hotel by one of your children while doing so. Do not be like Troy Maxson: be nice to your children, do not swing a baseball bat at your son, and let him live his life. Also, again, do not cheat on your spouse."

Comedy is not about the individual; comedy looks at the big picture. Comedy seeks to protect society from the excessive behavior of grandiose personalities. The characters are big, the actions are hefty, and as in the play *Something Rotten!*, the codpieces are capacious. Everything is exaggerated and because of their non-realistic approach, there are no individual consequences for the protagonists. Due to the audience's emotional and psychological detachment from the characters, the audience will focus on the lesson intended rather than worry about the fate of the individual caught up in comedic circumstances.

The lesson is: "Do not attack the family, as does Tartuffe, because society is composed of family units. If you destroy the family unit, society will crumble. Do not lie, be lazy, or have bad moral character as Jack does when he pretends to be Ernest. Blindly obeying artificial rules causes societal decay and so must be avoided. Do not be inflexible, as Felix and Oscar are to each other: all couples, no matter how odd, need to embrace each other's differences. Do not drink and drive as Homer Simpson and Peter Griffin do, for you will hurt or kill other people and destroy society one besotted car collision at a time. Drunk drivers can paralyze our transportation system and cause the collapse of our entire national economy."

The focus is never on the characters, but on their actions. In comedy, plot is everything. No matter what happens to the characters, audiences know that the characters will always be in fine fettle, and so audiences focus on the lesson and not the characters. Behind every comedic action there is a moral to the story. People may laugh when Captain Hook falls prey to the crocodile, but the lesson is that no one escapes the jaws of time. People may laugh when someone slips on a banana peel, but the writer is telling audiences to please put garbage in proper receptacles and watch your step.

The Greeks kept their tragedy out of their comedy and their comedy out of their tragedy. This was one of their rules for playwriting. Shakespeare was different from the Greeks in that he would sometimes insert comedic moments into his serious plays. Shakespeare's success is in part because of his dramatic use of juxtaposition. His plays like *King Lear* have parallel plots: one scene features Lear and the trouble he is having with his daughters and the next scene focuses on Gloucester and the trouble he is having with his sons. Another of Shakespeare's uses of juxtaposition is placing a funny scene right before the most serious moment in his play. This placement of comedy, when juxtaposed with the serious, by use of contrast and comparison maketh the serious or tragic scene appear to be even more tragic. The comedic juxtaposition intensifies the tragedy.

The characters Shakespeare used for these comedic scenes in his tragedies did follow Greek rules in one way, though, and that is that these comedic characters, like Greek comedic characters, were of the lower class and not the nobility, as Shakespeare's tragic lead characters tend to be. In *Hamlet,* Hamlet is the prince of Denmark. The comedic scene is between Hamlet and a couple of grave diggers. The grave diggers are laborers from the lower class. The scene, which is the next to last in the play, intensifies the final scene in which all the lead characters lose their lives. Hamlet is portrayed as being noble, heroic, and admirable, while the grave digger is an exaggerated comic clown stereotype.

In *Macbeth,* the comic character is the Porter, which is the equivalent of a butler, and a servant of lower class. Macbeth, in Act II, Scene 2, has murdered Duncan, the king. At the beginning of Act II, Scene 3, the Porter is awakened from his drunken sleep to answer knocking at the castle door. In his hungover misery he rails against all of society. He is an exaggerated comic stereotype, the drunk, and serves in stark contrast to the noble antihero, Macbeth. The Porter's drunken monologue of complaint, placed between the king's assassination and the discovery of the fell deed, increases the intensity of the tragedy, highlighting exactly how horrible are the actions of Lord and Lady Macbeth.

Shakespeare not only wrote serious tragedies and history plays, he also wrote actual comedies. Unlike the writers of Greek comedies, he used characters of the upper class as his protagonists, just as he did with his serious plays. In his comedies, there may have been similarities in the noble lead characters to the noble lead characters in Shakespeare's serious plays, but they were portrayed differently. A noble character in his comedy was not the same as a noble character in his serious play. One of the major differences was the use of language. The language in the comedies is not as heavy and dark; there is buoyancy and lightness to it. The use of language in a Shakespearean comedy conveys optimism, while the language used in his serious plays transmits a sense of pessimism.

In any comedy or serious dramatic work, whether it be Greek, Shakespearean, or contemporary, there is a key philosophical difference: tragedy is pessimistic, and comedy is optimistic. These philosophical opinions on the very nature of existence must be expressed in a unified manner in every aspect of the theatrical production. By looking at the set, costumes, makeup, hair, props, and lights, audiences should know if they are seeing a comedy or a serious play. This philosophy also needs to be expressed in the script and by its dramatization in the work of the actors. The style of language and its delivery, the facial expressions, gestures, body language, and movement technique of the tragic actor versus a comedic actor need to be different because they are expressing different messages that have different aspirations.

There is a difference in how the comedic actor's body moves as opposed to how the serious actor's body moves, and this brings me to the nexus of my argument as to why acting in a comedy is different from acting in a tragedy or serious play. In the acting theory that I espouse in this book, effective and good acting comes from a unified effort on the actor's part. In order for this effort to be unified, it must include the three major components of acting, which I have identified as the body, the mind, and the soul. In a tragedy, the philosophy, which comes from the soul, is the opposite of the philosophy or soul of a comedy. If the soul is different, then the body and the mind must be different. If the body moves differently in a comedy, then the mind and the soul need to follow the body in order to retain unity. The body is different in a comedy than it is in a tragedy; so too are the mind and the soul. Therefore, acting in a comedy must needs be different from acting in a serious play.

There are differences between acting in a comedy and acting in a serious play. What are these differences? Regarding the body, the physical laws that govern the characters are different in a comedy versus a tragedy, and so the body is affected. As to the mind, the goal of the serious actor is different from that of the comic, and so the methods for reaching those goals are different. Finally, for the soul, the energy and life philosophy are different for the two genres, and these differences have a great impact on everything the actor does.

The laws of physics are different in a comedy for the simple reason of the major law that rules comedy: there are never any serious consequences to potentially serious actions. No matter what happens in a slapstick comedy, audiences know the hero is going to be copacetic. The hero is hunky-dory because in a comedy the happy ending is guaranteed. If the protagonist is not okay, if the protagonist fails to achieve the superobjective, then the play is not a comedy. This removal of the possibility of serious harm causes the physical identity of the comedic character to be different from that of a tragic or serious character.

In a tragedy, there is a similar guarantee: there will always be serious consequences to serious actions. The absolute actuality that a character will die, or be horrifically maimed, or be directly responsible for the death of loved ones, coupled with the failure of the character to achieve a superobjective, is the hallmark of the classic tragedy. It is also still true for many contemporary serious plays, like *Sweat* by Lynn Nottage, *Dinner with Friends* by Donald Margulies, or *Disgraced* by Ayad Akhtar.

King Lear

These polar opposite differences need to be expressed physically by the actor. The actor should imagine that, when they are walking in a play, there is a chain attached to their waist. At the end of the chain is an anchor. In a tragedy, the anchor is sunk into the ground. The chain is taught, and to stand up, the actor must pull against it as the anchor tries to drown the actor in the earth. When the actor walks, the actor drags the anchor through the earth behind them.

In a comedy, the chain holding the anchor is still there, but the position of the anchor depends on the style of comedy the actor is performing:

Lesson 17—The Difference Between Tragic and Comedic Acting 143

a realistic comedy or a non-realistic comedy. In a realistic comedy, the anchor rests on the ground. It is still a drag on the actor, but not to nearly the extent that it is in a serious play. Walking still involves pulling the anchor behind the actor, but it is not as strenuous an activity as it is in a tragedy where the anchor is buried several feet into the ground.

In a non-realistic comedy, the actor is near weightless. The actor should imagine that the chain holding the anchor has been disconnected from them; the chain has dissolved, and the actor is free. Standing is an effortless activity, there is a boundless quality to the body, the actor seems nearly to hover above the ground rather than stand upon it, as though gravity has little claim over their infinitesimal mass. Walking for the actor is more like floating, as they flit from place to place while executing blocking with the greatest of ease.

This range—from heaviest, to least heavy, to weightlessness—needs to be expressed in other physical aspects of the actor. The posture of the actor in a serious play needs to illustrate the tug of the anchor. This is not to say that the tragic character should have bad posture. Characters in serious plays need to show that they carry the metaphorical weight of the world on their shoulders, that they are weighed down by their circumstances and hampered by the consequences of their choices. The shoulders can still be back; the chin can still be up; the chest can still be out. Audiences need to see, from heel to head's crown the pull of the chain expressed in the body, the effort it takes for the character to stand and move.

This heaviness and increase in levels of exertion to get even the slightest thing done also needs to be expressed in how the actor performs gestures. Even though the imagined chain is connected to the bottom center of the actor's torso, the pull of the chain is imagined to be experienced through the arms all the way down to the fingertips. The natural position for the arms, because a body at rest tends to stay at rest, is down by the body's side. Moving the arms takes massive effort. The arms are heavy and so the movements are slower, more ponderous. There are no extraneous movements in the arms or fingers because there is no spare energy to make those movements. Every physical gesture the actor makes, involving the entire arm down to the last inch of the longest finger, needs to be planned, choreographed, rehearsed, and executed flawlessly. In a tragedy or serious play, the gestures are akin to the words of the script: each one is specifically chosen for a reason; there are no extraneous or purposeless words. Dramatic language, even when written in prose, is condensed like poetry with no words wasted. The same quality needs to be imposed on the actor's physical movements, especially gestures and finger movements: nothing superfluous or purposeless because it takes so much energy and effort for the character to move.

Increased gravity and body density require increased effort for the slightest movement, so the speed at which a character moves in a serious play is slower than that of a comedic character. The decreased speed makes the movement more noble and stately, which helps identify classic tragic characters as the upper crust of society, as required by the Greeks and adhered to by Shakespeare. A tragic character is capable of rapid movement, but the level of muscle energy expenditure required to achieve it is so great that it can only occur in the most grievous of circumstances. Actors in a serous play need to move slower than actors in a comedic play.

Cumulatively, this added weight and expenditure of effort in a serous play tends to make the character appear weary and downtrodden. They can remain erect and continue to walk and move only because they are beings of immense power and cosmic stature. They face the big questions in life on behalf of the audience, and at the core of their being lies an essence of fatigue. Because of their exertion level, many of them are like Madeline Kahn's character in *Blazing Saddles*, and if they could, they would say as she does in her signature musical number, "I'm tired."

In the two types of comedy, realistic and non-realistic, the character's physical attributes the actor must portray are the opposite of those of the serious character. These physical attributes differ from each other only in the degrees of their oppositeness. If tragedy is at one end of the physicality pendulum's swing, non-realistic comedy is the farthest point of the swing away, and realistic comedy is about one-quarter of the way from non-realistic comedy's apex and three-quarters away from that of tragedy's farthest extremity.

The posture in non-realistic comedy is straight, erect, unless called for by the individuated demands of particular characters, and that erectness should appear effortless. There should be a carefree quality to the actor's physicality, in that the metaphorical weight of the world is not on them, that gravity is not pulling them down. Gravity is the force of the earth and life literally sucking the charac-

Uncle Vanya

ter further down into a clay embrace on the character's miserable journey to rejoin the dust from whence they came. There should be a spring in the comedic actor's step because of the character's lightness of being.

The actor enacting the gestures and body language of the comedic character needs to cut through the air with the greatest of ease. If in a serious play, the actor commits gestures as if they are underwater; in a comedy, the actor's gestures should be performed as though the character is miles above sea level, where the air is thin and arms can move through that air with nearly immeasurable ease. There needs to be quickness and lightness to the gestures. Arm movement and finger movement can be rapid and used with spontaneous regularity. With the proviso that hand and arm movement retain purpose and not distract from the actor's performance, there can be a more extemporaneous quality to the movement. The character is copiously animated, has more positive energy, and has a need to express happy things. Their movements are not all meant to express a struggle with life and death consequences because they are in a comedic world where everything always turns out okay.

Because of their lightness of being, the speed with which comedic characters move can be extravagantly more rapid and effortless than that of serious characters. Actors do not need to rush their movements, but rapid movement is more easily achievable than in a serious play.

Overall, there is a sense of energy to comedic characters. Because they live in a positive universe, comedic characters are not weighed down by dire circumstances and inevitability and can move without exerting much effort. Movement and life come easily for them. They still encounter obstacles, plot complications, opposing characters and conflict, but it is lavishly more in the vein of "It's all good fun," "It's not rocket science," and "It's not brain surgery." Because the characters comedic actors play are not dragging the anchors of their existence through the ground, because their bodies are not weighed down by an oppressive existence and there is little resistance to their physical movement, comedic characters do not have to expend as much energy to exist as do serious characters, and so comedic actors should have more energy, be more vital and not appear as though constantly physically exhausted, as actors playing serious characters may appear.

In my unified acting theory, where the body goes the mind must follow. The mind's responsibility for the actor includes assessing the character's superobjective. In addition to character goals, there are also actor goals. Actor goals are not the same as character goals. An actor in a serious play may want to make the audience think deep, philosophical thoughts on the play's main topic. An actor in a comedy play may have the goal of entertaining the audience and making them laugh.

Actors approach most serious plays and realistic comedies with the idea of doing the play *a la* realism. They may think that their actor goal is to convince the audience that they are not actors, they are their characters, to convince the audience that their characters are real. Perhaps a student's main exposure to acting has been through electronic entertainment media, like movies, television, or the web, with only minute exposure to stage acting. Acting teachers whose students largely work in film speak of "becoming the character" and making the work "real." The renowned Stella Adler (2000) writes of realism, "You play the play and you play the character to reveal the author's idea. You never play yourself. The actor's aim is to serve the theatre, never himself" (238). This can be taken to mean that actors must absent themselves from the experience, but without the actor there is no character and hence no play. Adler's advice is impractical, as everything is filtered through the actor; therefore, the actor must be present. Stage actors' objectives should never be to subtract themselves from their characters.

The stage actor who focuses only on convincing the audience that they are not there, that the actor is the character, is attempting to perform a magic trick. "No one up my sleeve, poof! Abracadabra! The character magically appears before your very eyes!" Stage magic does not include a magic actor. There is no such thing as a magic actor who is not there. The actor who says, "I am not here, I am the character and I do not exist," will not be believed by the audience. The audience knows that they are in a theater, watching actors on the stage. They know the actor is there and they do not want actors to lie to them; the audience does not like it.

Another phrase used in the magic actor theory of enacting serious plays or realistic comedies is called being "natural" on the stage. This is a term with which some noted performance theorists disagree. Cameron and Hoffman (1969), in their book *The Theatrical Response,* note:

> *Indeed, for as far back as at least the Restoration period, each dominant school of acting has defined itself as natural and the school which it has displaced as artificial; our own "technique" versus "method" controversy is a manifestation of the same split. In every age, actors who cannot fully master their instruments are inclined to label the work of those who can as "artificial." Confusing their egos with their creative imaginations, they are inclined to call their own work "natural"—meaning, it would seem that it is a manifestation of themselves rather than of an acquired set of gestures, rhythms, vocal patterns, and so on. Beneath this attitude, of course, is a misunderstanding of the nature of acting, a misunderstanding that has an equally limiting counterpart in the artificial or technical actor who has full control of his instrument but little or no ability to exercise his imagination. Whereas the first actor, the "natural," confuses his own feelings, his own ego, with creativity, the second actor confuses his own love of self-display, his desire for public exposure, with externalizing the role. (252–253)*

Lesson 17—The Difference Between Tragic and Comedic Acting 147

An actor may make it their goal to convince the audience that their character is a real person, but that goal will not engender in that actor their best work, not even when they are doing realism.

Audiences do not have to believe that a ballet dancer performing choreography is a character in order to enjoy the dance. Audiences can appreciate the skills of actors in the same way. Audiences exercising the willing suspension of disbelief are willing to let actors blind them with brilliant, skilled, and talented displays. Audiences want artistic beauty. To see real people in the theatre, they need merely turn their heads to look at other audience members. Audience members are the only real people in the theatre; on the stage there are only dramatic characters. It is like those commercials that post on-screen blurbs that describe the images as being "real people, not actors." Actors onstage are not people; they are dramatic characters.

The goal of the stage actor in a serious play as opposed to a comedy, then, is to make the audience engage their minds and think about the play's main idea and the questions the play poses about life, the universe, and everything. The goal of the actor in a comedy is to entertain the audience and make them laugh. The mind of the actor is influenced by the soul of the play, and the soul of a serious play is vastly different from the soul of a comedy.

Uncle Vanya

In the world of George Lucas, the differences in souls are expressed as the dark side and the light side of the Force. At least I guess it is the light side? They never actually name what the Jedi fight for, but if the opposition is the dark side, it makes sense to call it the light side. In moral terms, we refer to good versus evil, but no matter how you express it, it comes down to energy. The soul of the play, the play's philosophy, how the play views the world's nature, comes down to the presence of either positive or negative energy.

If the philosophical identity energy or soul of the play is positive, then it is optimistic. Comedy is optimistic because in the end everything is going to be all right. If everything is doomed, as it is in a tragedy, the philosophical identity energy or soul of the play is negative and pessimistic. I am an "optipest": the glass is half full, but the stuff probably tastes like crap, otherwise why didn't they drink the rest of it? Odom's Bar in Century, Florida, used to sell a shirt that read "Some people say the beer's half empty; some say the beer's half full. I say it's time to order another beer." That is entertaining, but when it comes to serious plays versus comedic plays, there is no optipestism; one is either optimistic or pessimistic, the glass is half full or it is half empty. The comedic actor needs to commit to positive energy and the tragic or serious actor needs to commit to negative energy.

Actors in comedies can express the play's positive energy through positive mannerisms in the body, face, and voice. Being in a serious play has a converse effect on actors' bodies, faces, and voices. This chapter has already covered the body, so on to the face. With positive energy, the face tends to smile more. Instead of resting grumpy face, the actor has resting happy face. The eyebrows are elevated and active, the eyes are open and bright, and the chin is effortlessly held high.

The voice of the comedic actor reflects positive energy through pleasing sounds. The voice is more upbeat and melodic, greeting other characters and situations with the expectation of a happy ending. In several works, David Mamet says that lines of dialogue in plays are not lines of dialogue, but actions the characters take upon other characters in order to achieve the superobjective. With that in mind, if the character did not want something, they would not speak. Since the energy of the play is positive, the character's voice reflects the expectation of victory, and so the character's voice need not be so infused with desperation.

Conversely, the face of the actor portraying a tragic or serious character reflects the negative energy of the play's world. There is a sense of impending doom in the character and so the face is less active, less fluid, stonier, and more grim. Resting grumpy face is common. The mouth is often turned down at the edges, the eyes are often squinty slits, and the eyebrows are furrowed in anger, concern, worry, or fear.

The characters, at least subconsciously, expect to lose. They feel trapped by circumstances, and this tension that pervades all their being is expressed in the sound of their voices. The tone is deeper, the quality has more gravel to it, and vocal variety exists but is on a smaller scale, the range more limited than with a comedic character. In many ways, the voice of the tragic actor is a somber voice of doom.

Lesson 17—The Difference Between Tragic and Comedic Acting

In conclusion, there is a difference when it comes to acting in a comedy versus acting in a tragedy or serious play. When approaching a performance, actors must first establish the style of comedy as being realism or non-realism. The same is true for serious plays, although most contemporary serious plays are rendered in the realistic style.

Tragic characters are larger than life in classical plays, and while comedic characters are meant to be quotidian, non-realistic characters depend on exaggeration to achieve comedic effect. The goals of serious plays and comedic plays are different in that serious plays seek to glorify mankind whereas comedies seek to degrade humanity. The philosophy of each genre is different and therefore the energy of each is different and must be expressed in an individuated manner by the actor in body, mind, and soul.

Exercise 1

1. Students should take a few minutes to think about their serious monologue, Monologue #2, and what adjustments they might make in order to perform it as a comedy. Students should not fear being wrong. This is just an exercise for fun, so take chances.
2. Volunteers take the performance space. Perform your serious monologue as a comedic one.

Exercise 2: Body

1. Students: imagine you are under water. You can breathe. Move about the space as though you are under water.
2. Students: walk about the room as a tragic character.
   A. Imagine the chain with the anchor plunged several feet down into the earth.
   B. Walk, dragging the anchor.
   C. Perform a series of gestures with the weight affecting your arms and hands. Illustrate the effort that moving through the water of existence takes from you.
3. Students: imagine the anchor is now resting on the ground instead of buried in it. The weight and pressure is less on your body, arms, fingers, and legs. You are on the ground at sea level instead of underwater. Repeat the series of movements from before: walking and gesturing. Express yourself with less effort and more positive energy.
4. Students: imagine the chain is broken. You are free. You are near weightless. You float from place to place and move your whole body with exuberance. It takes practically no effort because you are powerful, upbeat, and free. You are walking on the moon, literally and metaphorically.

Exercise 3: Face

1. Comedy face: Students will display various emotions through facial expression exercises. The professor will call out a series of emotions and students will portray them on their faces.
    A. Realism face: As the professor calls out emotions, students make the faces as they would when doing realistic comedy.
    B. Non-realism: As the professor calls out emotions, students make the faces as they would when doing non-realistic comedy.
2. Serious face: Students will display various emotions through facial expressions. As the professor calls out emotions from a tragedy play, students will show these tragic emotions on their faces.

Exercise 4: Voice

1. Volunteers: The class will hear readings of students' comedic monologues, reflecting the style of the piece and the positive energy through the voice.
2. Students should practice with their comedy face as they read.
3. Students should determine if the piece is realistic comedy on non-realistic comedy. The class can help with this determination.

Lesson 18
Monologue #3 Rehearsal

Exercise 1

1. Comedy monologue rehearsal day. If the student has blocking prepared, please show the class. Today the class needs to have all students perform their pieces twice.
   A. The first time is to get a feel for the piece and to evaluate the actor's staging, blocking, body language, gestures, and business.
   B. The second time is after improvements have been made to actor staging.
   C. In the absence of actor blocking, the professor will help the actor stage the piece.
2. The class will watch each student perform and critique/contribute to the construction of each performance. Everyone is responsible for the successful staging of everyone else's monologue.

Homework

Students should be off-book for Monologue #3, comedic monologue, next class.

Lesson 19
Day Two
Monologue #3 Rehearsal

Exercise 1
1. This is an off-book rehearsal for everyone.
2. All students are to watch and, if requested, contribute criticism to classmates' performances.
3. Each actor will perform the piece twice: once, then receive feedback, then again incorporating feedback as improvements in the performance.

Acting I Monologue #3 Evaluation

Name _____

Timing _____

Date _____

Scoring 5 - Superior
4 - Excellent
3 - Good
2 - Fair
1 - Poor

Positive Energy
1   *   2   *   3   *   4   *   5

Exaggerations
1   *   2   *   3   *   4   *   5

Facial Expressions
1   *   2   *   3   *   4   *   5

Vocal Inflections
1   *   2   *   3   *   4   *   5

Gestures
1   *   2   *   3   *   4   *   5

Blocking
1 * 2 * 3 * 4 * 5

Memorization
1 * 2 * 3 * 4 * 5

Commitment
1 * 2 * 3 * 4 * 5

Projection
1 * 2 * 3 * 4 * 5

Remarks:

Grade

Lesson 20
Monologue #3 Performance

1. The class will perform vocal and physical warm-ups
2. Class members should take notes on each performance.
   A. Bring these notes back to class.
   B. The class will hear everyone's notes aloud.
   C. Strive to identify two strengths and two weaknesses for each performer.
3. When it is the student's turn, the student takes the space and waits until the professor signals to begin.
4. After each performance, the professor will finish making notes. The next performer can take the space, but should not begin until the professor has finished evaluating the previous performer and is ready to evaluate the next.
5. The professor will take the notes made today and after class use them to formulate student grades. The professor will disseminate grade sheets next class.
6. Once everyone has performed, the class will create the Circle of Feedback.
   A. In the Circle of Feedback, the class arranges the furniture into a circle.
   B. The professor will navigate the circle and discuss, in order, each performance.
   C. First the class discusses strengths, anything the class believes the actor did well.
   D. Next the class discusses weaknesses, areas of improvement for the actor.
   E. If there are conflicting or confusing notes, please discuss after class or during office hours with the professor.

Lesson 21
Working with Others
Everybody Farts

Exercise 1: Meet and Greet
1. Students should line up desks so that everyone sits facing someone else. There should be a line of desks stretching from one end of the classroom to the other, with two lines of students sitting facing each other over the desks from both sides. The people sitting across from each other are now partners.
2. Students have ninety seconds to tell each other about themselves. Person 1, talk about yourself to Person 2 for ninety seconds, before the professor calls stop. Then Person 2, talk about yourself to Person 1 for ninety seconds.
3. Professor calls "next." Students should change partners. For the first change, the people who were on the side where Person 1 sat, move down one chair. Person 2 should stay in place. For the next change, Person 2 should move in the opposite direction while Person 1 stays in place, and so on. Continue until the original Person 1 is back to their original Person 2.
4. Repeat, only this time each student tells their partner about themselves for sixty seconds.
5. Repeat, only this time students tell partners about each other for thirty seconds.

One Thanksgiving, as we were sitting down to the feast, my brother was commiserating about one of his coworkers, about how awful this guy was at his job, and that if his boss did not start making this guy pull his weight and do his job, my brother was going to quit. My mother and I rolled our eyes because my brother, a sixty-year-old person, has been this exact same way at every job he has ever had in his whole life. This is usually true with every job anyone has ever had: there is always at least one person with whom you work who you cannot stand to work with and wish that they would just go away.

It is a fact of life that the world is full of people and with so many people, there are always people you like and people you dislike. This is in line with the Serenity Prayer thing, in which you accept the things you cannot change. You cannot go around the world enacting change on everyone you dislike, changing the behaviors of everyone who does something that irritates you. You cannot change the behavior of other people because you cannot control other people. The only person you can control is yourself.

One reason a person may want to change another person is because Person 1 believes that their way of seeing and doing things is superior to the ways that other people see and do things. If Person 1 always leaves the toilet seat down, it may boggle their mind and infuriate them that some people leave the toilet seat up. Person 1 may always use their turn signal when navigating traffic and become filled with road rage when other people driving near them do not. Sure, the way Person 1 does things works for them; that is why Person 1 does it that way. But what Person 1 may not realize is that the way Person 1 does things is merely Person 1's opinion about how things should be done. What works for Person 1 may not necessarily work as well for other people, and so those other people may have worked out other ways of doing things that they, in turn, believe are superior to the way Person 1 does things. And gladly or sadly, all these people are simultaneously right and wrong.

Spamalot

While it is important that actors have confidence in themselves and their abilities, it is not necessary that they be egomaniacal monsters. While the nature of acting is at its heart competitive, the instinctive goal of the actor should not be to destroy their inferior partner and to shame them into submission. The actor should remember that they are not, in fact, all that and a bag of chips. I was discussing this chapter topic with some fellow educators, and one teacher suggested the title of this chapter should actually be, "You Aren't Special and You Still Smell So You Better Check Your 'Tude." Another friend said the title should just be "Play Nice."

These two suggestions imply that for an actor to work successfully with other actors, they must be humble. They must also realize that we are all humans and that we all suffer from human weaknesses that must be regularly addressed. Because of this, actors are respectful and polite to other people, always making productive conversational and behavioral choices that are pleasing to the other actors. In other words: everybody farts. You fart, your partner farts, everybody farts, and we all work within each other's cloud bursts. To end with a metaphor of a different color, life is a public pool and not everyone obeys the signs about bathroom breaks.

An actor does not just work with other actors, however. The actor works with three main categories, or distinct groups of people, each representing a different form of relationship in which the actor must be successful. The actor works firstly with the audience, secondly with directors, and thirdly with other actors. Furthermore, in a fully realized production, the actor works with the technical stage crew.

Theatre actors work with an audience. The actor-audience relationship is extremely complicated. Often in human relationships there is a dominant partner and a submissive partner, a leader and a follower, a queen and a worker bee. In the relationship between actor and audience, who is the dominant party?

Exercise 2

1. Class should divide into two groups.
2. Group 1 is assigned the audience. Group 2 is assigned the actor.
3. Each group develops an argument that supports their position that their group is the dominant party in the relationship. Each position must contain several valid supporting reasons.
4. Each group takes turns reporting their position to the rest of the class.

One can argue that they are equal, but this is not true. The audience has paid the actors to perform. Does this make the actor the audience's employee? Or, one might say that the audience so wants to be in the presence of the actor that the audience has paid for the privilege, a privilege the actor may revoke by leaving at any moment. Still, an actor who walks out on performances will not continue to sell tickets, and with no ticket sales, how will the actor continue to earn money to pay rent and buy groceries? As long as money is involved, the audience has power, but for the performance experience to be successful, the audience must be willing to cede that power to the actor, with the proviso that should the actor fail to please the audience, they will take that power back. This is a complicated relationship indeed, one that Alec Baldwin, Sissy Spacek, and Dame Judi Dench have commented upon in their autobiographies.

Alec Baldwin splits his career between stage work and working in front of a camera. In the following passage, he speaks of the camera but what he says is equally applicable to live audiences. Baldwin (2017) speaks of a lesson he learned from cinematographer Donald Peterman:

> *The first lesson he taught me is that the camera is the real star of every movie, and your first priority as a film actor is to get your relationship right with it. How you have prepared, how you look, how truthful you and the choices you make for your character are only matter if they are revealed to the camera. Otherwise, it's like painstakingly crafting a painting only to hang it on the wall backwards. (111)*

The primary relationship in theatre is that of the audience and the actor—not the relationship between two actors in a scene. If two actors play a brilliant scene but the audience does not see or hear it, then it might as well have never happened. Theatre is not born until the audience arrives. The actors exist to communicate the script to the audience. Therefore, it is the actor's responsibility to make sure that the audience perceives their actions as dramatically successful and aesthetically pleasing. Successful acting escapades require vocal and physical attributes that are carefully designed and perfected with scrupulous, rigorous rehearsals. The actor needs to be aware of how they look and sound to the audience and how best to position themselves to maximize dramatic potency.

Baldwin (2017) addresses this ability when he writes:

> *Like nearly all good film actors I have worked with, over time I developed an innate, acute sense of how to adjust for the camera. The job was to act with others in a scene, but also, to the best of my ability, factor in the camera and, thus, the audience itself. The camera is the proscenium, and I always feel compelled to triangulate my performance with it and the other actors. Wherever the camera is, I'll unconsciously adjust to it. (181)*

I believe Baldwin has hit on a perfect description. Baldwin translates the concept from acting for the camera to the stage by using the metaphor of the camera as the proscenium arch, the opening that frames and separates the actor from the audience. The audience sits behind the proscenium and watches the action. His term "triangulating" the action dovetails nicely with my description of every scene being at least a three-person scene between you, your acting partner, and the audience, with the need to keep all three points of the triangle fully engaged.

No matter the style, even the realest of realisms, the actor cannot ignore the audience because they are an indelible factor of the acting. A connection is needed between the actor and audience. Baldwin describes his adjustments as being unconscious, but that is only because he has been acting for decades. At the beginning of an actor's career, it starts as a very conscious process. Spacek (2012) describes the kind of connection actors need to seek with audiences: "I began to understand that the art forms that excited me most were those that illuminated the human condition, explored our shared experience, and connected us in some way." She sought a connectedness in acting similar to the emotional connection between a singer in concert and the audience, where the audience "was *right there with me,* feeling what I was feeling" (121–122).

Singers with live audiences have an advantage over actors with a live audience; that advantage is music. Music causes an emotional reaction in people. Actors in straight plays can achieve the same level of connection even without music. The quality of the feeling is different; without music the feeling is more intellectual. The audience does not just hear the actor's voice saying the dialogue and react emotionally. They have to hear the ideas behind the words and go on the emotional journey with the character. When these are all combined, the audience can feel emotions and bond with the actor in a play the same way they do with a singer in concert.

Something wonderful happens with the audience that confers a behemoth-sized responsibility on the actor. When a multitude of people—be it dozens, hundreds, or thousands—experience an emotion at the same time, the phenomenon of all those people feeling the same thing at the same time magnifies the emotion's intensity. At home alone, a person might just give a little chuckle at a joke, but at the theatre with hundreds of other people, the chuckle intensifies into a belly laugh. At home alone, a person might just go, "Aw," when something sad happens, but embedded in the throng, the person may cry genuine tears. It is this intensification that is responsible for that theatre advertising slogan, "You'll laugh, you'll cry, it'll become a part of you." The leviathan responsibility on the actor is that they are the leader of this experience. This is a position of great power that must not be misused.

The performance, however, is for the audience, not the actor. As people, we can never truly know how we look and sound to others because we are trapped by our own beliefs of what we look and sound like. The actor realizes that they will never know what their performance looks like to the

Spamalot

audience. They cannot, because they are up on the stage and can never be in the house at the same time. Dench (2010) touches on this when she writes about watching her production of *Macbeth* that was recorded for television: "I made the great mistake of watching it, and I was desperately disappointed in what I had done. I had imagined that my performance was better than what I saw on the screen. It stopped me watching anything else" (79).

Her performance was designed for the live audience and not for the camera; that is why she perceived it to be so bad. No matter how well it is recorded, no taping of a live play performance will ever be as good as it was for the live audience. What happens onstage can never be captured by camera, which is why if you ever watch a play you were in on video, you, like Dench, will most likely be deeply disappointed in the quality. It never looks good on video. Therefore, actors can never know the truth about their performance quality and effectiveness. This is why God—and producers—made directors, and it is important that actors have good relationships with directors. Actors work with directors.

A very important working relationship for actors is the one they have with the director, or in the case of an acting class, the professor. All people are created equal and no one should bully or be bullied, but in the workplace, there is always a chain of responsibility. A producer decides to mount a play production. The producer selects a script. The producer hires a director. The director analyzes the script and creates the director's interpretation of that script to be used for the production. The director works with designers, technicians, and actors to communicate that director's vision to the audience. In all things, the director is the executive artist responsible for every aspect of the production. If a director is lucky, they hire good people and get out of the way. The best productions are often the ones in which the director does scant creative work. In a literary comparison, the actors and other artists are the writers and the director is the editor.

In the professional world—the model for community theatre and the destination for artists getting their theatrical education—the director is the person in charge, the actor's immediate workplace supervisor. In the academic industry, there is a chain of command. Artistic decisions can be discussed during the analytical and rehearsal stages, but once a decision is made, the role of the actors and artists is to communicate the director's interpretation of the experience to the audience. The producer trusts the director who trusts the designers and actors. Professional decorum demands that respect roll both ways, with actors trusting their directors' choices.

Ultimately a director's choice is an artistic opinion. The actor has artistic opinions, too. The actor may believe that their artistic opinion is superior to that of the director. Most likely the director feels the same way about their artistic opinion. But if the director disagrees with the actor, the actor is expected to follow the director's vision, because the director is the workplace supervisor. A friend of mine, Stan Dean, used to tell me, "When you're the director, we'll do it your way." For the actor-director relationship to work, the actor must trust the director. That is part of the actor's employment contract: to trust the director. Dame Judi Dench (2010) touches on this when she describes working on an improvised script for director Robert Altman: "As actors we were all thrilled to be working with such an innovative director, and we gave the film everything we had, even when we weren't sure what we were doing" (178).

What if the actor fundamentally disagrees with the director? I once had a student—I'll call him Willy—ignore my advice for a scene we were working on in class. I asked Willy to not play directly to the professor just because the professor was grading the scene. Willy said no, because Willy wanted the professor to get the maximum impact of the performance. Willy would make eye contact with the professor because that's the way Willy thought it should be done. Willy said, "It doesn't matter how many degrees you have, or how many years of experience you have, that does not mean you are always right." I said okay.

Willy had strong personal feelings about the choice to demand, in a realistic scene, that the professor make eye contact with Willy and in essence, perform the scene with Willy, despite the fact that Willy had a scene partner with whom the scene was meant to be shared. Willy's classmates informed Willy that playing just to the professor made the scene look fake and in the Circle of Feedback gave him the same weakness note over and over. Willy came to me later and expressed regret for not heeding the advice of the class. Willy had thought the professor was wrong and so ignored my suggestions. Willy was correct in that I am not always right. I have been wrong often in my life and have probably made every mistake that an actor can make onstage in front of an audience. And I learned from each of those instances what not to do, what to avoid, what makes a choice strong and what makes a choice weak. To ignore a professor's extensive training and experience can be a mistake on the part of the student actor. When it comes to an acting choice in class, the professor's opinion is meant to help the student earn a better grade on performance day. If the professor tells the student that a choice is weak, or to please look for a stronger choice, for the sake of growth perhaps the student can try it that way. The great thing about the performing arts is that you never have to settle for a performance; there's always a revival.

Most directors and professors have extensive training and years of experience in theatre. If a student does not know something, they should ask the director or professor. Most of them will be happy to regale students with the story of their career and how they came to be working with you at that moment. The actor has to trust the director's choices, as Dench (2010) points out when discussing director Frank Hauser: "He was very intelligent, witty, funny, and precise. Tall and lean, he worked hard, and had such an insight into everything to do with the theatre. I once said that if Frank asked me to step in front of a bus I'd do it. I'd know he had some good reason" (34). That level of faith is nice.

Let us say, though, that it is not always possible. As an actor, I have disagreed with a few directors on rare occasions. The worst was a full-blown argument I had before the assembled cast during notes after the final dress rehearsal of *Bye Bye Birdie* at my high school. In my defense, I was only in the tenth grade and had no idea how little I knew. I wish I could go back in time and spank me; I was such a punk. The director was criticizing the cast for not working hard enough. I was confused because I had worked my aft off—how could he tell me I was not working hard enough? Turns out, he was not talking to me. That never even occurred to me. But before the director could pull me aside and tell me that, I had retaliated. It was awful! Please be better than me and never do that. I apologized to him in person after I "grew up," but still, to Dayton Long, my high school director: I was wrong, and I am sorry.

If actors do not have complete faith in their directors, too bad, so sad, the director is still the workplace supervisor. As Jack Nicholson explains when he talks about working with director Vincente Minnelli on a movie that he hated, "I've got twelve years' experience in all phases of filmmaking. I did please Vincente Minnelli because in my own theory of acting, I must please the director, and I think Minnelli is good, but each night [of shooting] I was unhappy" (Eliot 2013, 74). Jack was unhappy, but saw it as his job as an actor to make the director happy.

Compartmentalization of responsibility is a good thing. The actor's performance creates positive energy in the director. It is the director's job to please the audience. The producer decides if the director has pleased the audience, and if so, the director gets to continue their directing career. While an actor can disagree with a director, it is up to the producer and ultimately the audience as to whether the director is doing a good job.

The final group of people that actors work with is the most challenging because that group is composed of other actors. At this point I want to note that when I crack jokes about actors, I am including myself. It is like how it is okay for me to make bald jokes because I am follicularly challenged. I joke because I love.

Actors are people, and just like other people, actors can be cruel, stupid, overemotional, thoughtless, egotistical, self-centered, impractical, lazy, snobbish, rude, and elitist. And those are the good ones. But they can also be the absolute best people who ever lived in the history of all people everywhere. Regardless, as actors, students in this class will work with other actors. While no two actors, like snowflakes, are exactly alike and some are flakier than others, there are no rules that dictate how to work with everyone. All actors are human, however, so they have enough in common with each other that there are some recommended behaviors that will serve student actors well and decrease the difficulty of working with other actors.

Theatre people should be kind to each other. In a production, this includes other actors as well as crew members. We are all one team and should all be nice to each other. Niceness includes leaving all negativity outside of the workplace. Dame Judi Dench (2010) advises people to leave their baggage offstage.

> It is rather a harsh lesson to learn, but nevertheless it is no good saying, oh, my father died or something, and I don't feel like it. This is not what the audience ever comes to see, they come to see that particular story and how you interpret it. So you have to learn to put those things in a little side-compartment sometimes, and draw on them when you need them. (19)

Actors should not be self-indulgent; they realize that the scene or play is not about them. It is about the team, even and especially if it is a small team comprised of only two actors.

When you work with other people, you are in close proximity to each other. The rehearsal or performance space may be a classroom, a small stage, or a big mainstage space, but often scenes between two characters bespeak a certain intimacy. An actor may be called upon to touch, hug, kiss, or even simulate extreme physical intimacy. For this reason, it is imperative that actors maintain good hygiene. Actors should bathe or shower daily. Use antiperspirant deodorant, but avoid heavy perfumes or colognes, especially in large, overpowering doses. Change clothes on a regular basis. Actors may think the clothes they wore yesterday are good for another day, but the clothes carry the smell of yesterday . . . *all* the smells of yesterday. Do laundry on a regular basis and change clothes daily. Finally, actors need to maintain good oral hygiene, especially if a scene involves talking directly into another actor's face or kissing. If you eat right before rehearsal or performance, which is ill-advised, remember that your mouth and breath carry your repast for some time after your final swallow. If you cannot brush your teeth again, how about a rinse, with either water or, hopefully, the mouthwash that you should keep in a locker or backpack. If all else fails, you can always eat a mint, like a Tic Tac or two. Probably at least two. Who only uses one Tic Tac?

I saw a post on Facebook from an actor named Laura Sebastian and she had some good observations about actors working with other people. She wrote:

> I love working with actors who know how to do their job without making it hard for the director or other actors, or anyone else. Yes, those actors are fun to be on stage with: the ones who do their jobs without a fuss, without telling you how to do yours, or make the director spend inordinate amounts of time and energy on them. Yes. Those actors make the work a pleasure. I've worked with lots of them. It raises the whole experience. I've been that kind of actor. I've also been an ass as an actor. . . . Never again! I recently learned my lesson. That kind of actor is exhausting and I hate working with them!

A good actor is someone who knows their job—they know basic acting technique; they have prepared for the role. The good actor works well with the director, other actors, and all other personnel. The good actor does not demand the director follow the actor's process at the expense of the rest of the cast. The good actor realizes that directors are human. The good actor, as Sebastian says, does not behave like "an ass."

One thing she says that stands out as especially relevant for an Acting I class is that good actors do not tell their acting partners how to do their job, or how other actors should play their parts. Actors should not direct other actors. One actor should not tell another actor how to play a part. In this class, student actors might be tempted to give advice to their acting partners. Avoid the temptation. Let them do their job and you do yours. Acting is a very intimate thing and getting between actors and their parts can irreparably damage working relationships. Rita Moreno (2013) describes an incident that happened while she was working on *West Side Story* that gives an idea of the intimacy of actor and character.

When I had to play the attack scene in the candy store, I wept and broke down—right on set. It was that incredible, amazing, magical thing that happens sometimes when you're acting and you have the opportunity to play a part so close to your heart: you pass through the membrane separating your stage self from your real self. For a time, at least, you are one person. (183)

Actors do not intrude on someone else's artistic experience. The actor's golden rule is "do unto your acting partner as you would have your acting partner do unto you."

This does not mean students can never offer a partner advice, especially if they ask for it. But if you, as a student actor, feel compelled to give unsolicited advice, carefully examine it before you offer it. It may be something you should keep to yourself. Store it away, and if there is ever a day when you get to play that character in that scene, use your own advice for yourself.

In This Class

Here is some advice specifically finagled for this class and the scenes students will be doing the rest of this semester. The following exercise is meant to elucidate what it means to "be nice" to someone:

Exercise 3

1. Think-Pair-Share: An exercise in which the professor introduces a topic and each student thinks alone about the topic, then partners with another student. The students in each pair discuss their individual ideas on the topic and attempt to come to a consensus. Then each pair will share their mutual effort aloud with the rest of the class at the professor's direction.

   A. <u>Topic 1</u>: In your opinion, what are characteristics that you like in people, behaviors that lead you to define someone as being a "good person" or a "nice person"?

   B. <u>Topic 2</u>: In your opinion, what makes a person a good acting partner? If applicable, students can share examples from their lives of experiences in which people were nice or good.

   C. <u>Topic 3</u>: In your opinion, what are characteristics and behaviors that are unlikable in people, that lead you to define someone as a bad person?

   D. <u>Topic 4</u>: In your opinion, what makes a person a bad acting partner? If applicable, students can share experiences from their own lives in which someone has done something that filled them with loathing, where someone did them wrong.

2. If the class examines their responses to the discussion topics, the class can create a list of behaviors worthy of emulation. Conversely, the class can create a list of behaviors that should be assiduously avoided. Students should remember these as they work on scenes with acting partners.

Exercise 4

Students, today you will be assigned your first acting partner. The professor has taken each of your names and written them down on small pieces of paper. The professor has folded these pieces of paper and placed them in a receptacle such as a hat or toy bucket. I call mine the Bucket of Chaos. The professor will stir and shake the contents of the Bucket of Chaos to ensure that the assignment of partners is completely random and designed only by blind fate. The professor will now draw student names.

Once students have been assigned partners, each student should visualize working with their partner as the professor enumerates advised behavioral patterns.

1. Do not try to dominate your partner and force them into doing the line or scene the way you want them done. Your partner has ideas too, possibly ideas of which you would never have thought, and can provide fresh input. You cannot learn from yourself, as you already know everything that you know. You can only learn new information from other people, so be prepared to gain enrichment from your partner.

2. Do not try to get your partner to do the scene the way you saw it in your head when you were working alone. Neither you nor your partner is the director; you are equals. Rehearsal is for unifying through compromise the ideas of both you and your partner. Manipulating your partner into doing the scene the way you imagined it rules out your partner's contribution and can result in stale, uninspired, and barren performances.

3. Do not let your acting colleague bully you or push you around. I have held classes where actors thought they knew everything and that their way was the only possible way to do the scene. Their cohort might have disagreed, but were shy, easily dominated, and acquiesced despite misgivings. Do not be afraid to stand up for yourself and, if necessary, use the professor as a mediator if you and your collaborator cannot come to an agreement or if your chum will not behave.

4. This class is supposed to be a positive experience for everyone. Alan Arkin (2011) once wrote, "And I began to realize that the underlying message that runs through all of the group art forms, whether it be dance, music, theater, or film, is: 'Look at us! We can get along! We can do this beautiful thing and we are doing it together and actually enjoying each other! There is hope for us after all!'" (92). So be the hope, be the joy by remembering it is not about you or your partner—it is about both of you. You are a team, working together, which is why it is known as teamwork.

5. Respect each other, which in this case means doing the work. When lines are due, you should have them memorized. When actors ask me, "When are lines due, when are we supposed to be off-book?" I tell them that "Lines are due now." If you have the part in hand, why would you pro-

crastinate on memorization? Memorize immediately because true acting only begins once you can put the script down.

6. Respect means learning the blocking. When the two of you block the scene, write it down. Study the blocking along with the lines so that from rehearsal to rehearsal you are not completely changing the agreed upon blocking to which your partner expects you to adhere. It is amazingly frustrating when an actor has studied the blocking, but their acting partner has not and makes up their movements anew each time they go over the scene. It can be really infuriating and detrimental to the clarity and quality of the scene's physicality upon performance. Also, it can cost you your positive relationship with your classmates should you disrespect them in this manner.

7. If an actor is difficult to work with and they abuse either greatly or infinitesimally their scene partner, the rest of the class may notice. The abusive actor may even be the subject of unkind gossip outside of class. If this happens, no one will want to be the abusive actor's partner for the second scene. No one will want to play with an actor who does not play nice.

8. Respect the class in general. If you are cast in a show and are working hard at rehearsals but shirking your classwork, the message that you send is that the class, and by extension your classmates, are inconsequential and trifling. Do in class as you do in production. Your work is always a reflection of who you are. If an actor behaves like a lazy snit in class, word may get around and a future director, torn between casting the lazy snit and someone else, may hear that the lazy snit's work ethic is questionable and therefore decide not to take a chance on that actor. Actors are expected to do the work. It is understood that actors will memorize. Memorization for an actor is like breathing for all life forms: it is part of you and necessary.

9. Respecting each other also means working together outside of class time. If class time is the only occasion acting partners unite to work on the scene, they are not doing their jobs. Demand that your partner rehearses with you outside of class. Early on, exchange contact information and agree on a system of communication: text, phone, email, Facebook, Instagram, or whatever. Compare schedules and make rehearsal appointments. Then keep the appointment. Both of you. Homework for this class consists of the following:

   A. Research your scene.
   B. Analyze your scene.
   C. Memorize your scene.
   D. Rehearse your scene.

Rehearsing outside of class is required homework. Not doing so results in an under-rehearsed scene that consequently may have a poor performance grade. Good grades require work.

After you have researched, analyzed, and memorized the dialogue, early rehearsals include blocking the scene. Acting partners should block the scene together. The next chapter focuses on the mechanics of blocking, which we'll discuss more later. Once you have finished designing your physical performance, the actors rehearse the scene over and over and over. No matter how many times you do the scene, however, it needs to retain that freshness, that illusion of the first time. The chapter after next covers repeat performances, so more on that even later, but for now, one sure way to safeguard the vividity of your scene work is to listen to each other.

Listening to each other does not mean that actors wait for their partner to quit speaking and then take their turn at elocution. It is not even merely hearing the words. Listening means hearing the words, how they are said, and reacting to the actual intent and energy the other actor is giving in the moment. The way one partner says the line customizes the other partner's response. If they say, "I love you" in a way that conveys the opposite meaning, perhaps with no energy or even with a trace of hostility, respond to that energy, not just the words. The actor's customized reaction will in turn affect their partner, and this moment-by-moment exchange of energy will bring the scene to turbulent life. It is like Betty White (2011) says: "You have to listen and play off what someone else says. You can't be thinking of what you're going to say next or it dies right there. If you listen to people, it triggers something in you to which you can respond. It's about both really listening and hearing that funny track that you can pick up and deliver back." She goes on to say, "I can't tell you it's innate. . . . But I think you have to have a propensity for it. And after that, practice helps a lot" (137).

Particularly relevant is her use of the term "trigger." While an actor listens to their partner say their line, the actor is not just listening for their line cue. A line cue is the word their partner's character says that signals the actor to say their line. The line cue is usually the other character's last word. In addition to listening for the line cue, the actor is also listening for what I call the trigger word. The trigger word is the word or phrase that the other character says that makes your character feel a command to respond. It may be the last word, like the line cue, but it just as easily might not be. For example, look at a brief excerpt from Act I of my play, *The Vinyl Id*. In this scene, Kiljoy, a stand-up comic, is entering a diner. She is pursued by the diner's male manager who is upset with her because he feels she has parked illegally in his parking lot.

Lesson 21—Working with Others 169

KILJOY enters, followed by a yelling restaurant MANAGER

(1) MANAGER
Miss, I told you!

(2) KILJOY
And I told you, do I look like a little girl? You stop calling me "miss." I am **woman,** hear me roar.

(3) MANAGER
Woman, you can't **park** there!

(4) KILJOY
I *am* **handicapped**. You see me limping, don't you?

(5) MANAGER
You don't have a handicap **tag or decal** or anything!

(6) KILJOY
Rules, rules, rules. You know why men like rules? Because they **suck** more than anything.

(7) MANAGER
I'm calling the **cops!**

(8) KILJOY
Go ahead, my dad's a cop. I hope he shoots you dead!

In the first line, the Manager's word "Miss" is the trigger word for Kiljoy's first line. Hearing that word drives her to reply. At that point, the actor can inhale and be ready to speak as soon as they hear their cue word. In line #2, Kiljoy's word "woman" serves as the trigger word for the Manager's next line, line #3. In that line, the Manager's word "park" is Kiljoy's next trigger. In line #4, when Kiljoy says "handicapped," that serves as the Manager's next trigger. In line #5, the Manager's word "decal" is Kiljoy's next trigger. The "tag or decal" are artifacts that represent the "rules" that she rails against in line #6, where Kiljoy's use of the word "suck" triggers the Manager's response. For one, he is offended by the sexual tone of the word as used in his workplace, and two, he sees that she is not inclined to obey the law because of her staunch disapproval of it. Finally, in line #7, the Manager's word "cops" serves as the trigger word. As it is the last word in the line, it is also the line cue, showing that while the trigger word may not always be the same as the line cue, it can be.

Careful analysis of the script to identify the character's trigger words will guarantee that the actor is actively listening to their partner. It also makes it much more likely that both actors will pick up their line cues because it imbues their character with an impatient quality and a strong desire to say the next line. The characters can hardly wait to say it. This imbues the scene with forward momentum and energy, making it crackle with life.

Whether it is working with audiences, directors, crew members, or other actors, working with others is a complex undertaking. The main requirements are patience and understanding. Actors should remember that both they and their partners are only human. Everybody farts. Everybody's farts stink. Hope for patience and understanding if you butt yodel near your partner and be sure to extend it if your partner butt yodels near you.

Homework

Students should bring a scene to the next class with a copy for each partner and one for the professor. The scene should be five to seven minutes long in running time. The scene should be from a published play for the stage and should be a tragic or serious scene.

Spamalot

Lesson 22
Blocking a Scene
No, Stage Right. The Other Stage Right!

Noises Off

You may ask yourself, "Self, why do I have to learn how to block a scene? Isn't that what directors are for?" And yourself might answer, "Why do you keep asking me questions?" The answer is that blocking is a marvelous skill for an actor to cultivate. Learning how to block a scene will prepare actors for directing classes, but even more importantly, it instills in students an invaluable ability to be used in future acting classes. It is highly recommended that actors in this class continue to take acting classes because an actor's education is never complete. Actors never reach a point where they know everything and will never learn anything ever again. As students continue to take acting classes, they will need to know how to block scenes. As an example, I will use our Acting II class that is offered at Pensacola State College.

In Acting II, over the semester students must perform four scenes, each scene from a different acting style. Usually there is a Greek scene, a Shakespearean scene, a realism scene, and a post-realism scene, often theatre of the absurd or dramatic prose poetry like that of Harold Pinter or Paula Vogel. There are discussions of theory and the execution of exercises at the beginning of each section, but most of the class is rehearsing the scenes and learning through practical, experiential events. Part of the rehearsal process for students is to create their own blocking for the scenes. The professor gives feedback and aid as required, but the initial blocking comes from the students' own creativity.

Often in acting classes, actors are left to their own devices in blocking and otherwise preparing scenes. The professors in future acting classes at accredited colleges and universities will want to see the scene without giving students extensive help in preparing it. The professor wants to view the scene and then give the students feedback, offering direction and advice on how they can improve the scene and what they should be learning in the process. The initial creation of the scene will be up to the student actors.

While this is true in higher learning, it is especially true for acting classes at unaccredited schools or organizations where students can get private acting lessons. Whether it be a nonprofit organization like a local theatre, a private individual, or a company that offers acting lessons, if student actors are working on a scene, the organization or teacher expects the students to prepare the scene and bring it to class so that they can work on it with the students. These future acting classes are good reasons for students in this class to learn the basics of how to block a scene, but wait, there's more!

The directors that student actors in this class will work with in future productions, for instance, may be the kind of directors who do not plan scenes and therefore show up at rehearsal with no blocking to give the cast. This kind of director likes to create the blocking with the actors at rehearsal and may say to an actor, when it is time to block the show, "Let's see what happens, just move when and where the urge to move hits you." When I was a beginning actor, the only urge to move I experienced when told this by a director was the urge to run away from the pressure of creating blocking on the spot. I instantly became so self-conscious. I wanted to exit the theatre and go back to drawing my own comic books. I was an inexperienced actor; I did not know when or how or where to move. I was a teenager, for Pete's sake, and who the heck is Pete, anyway? In order to be ready to work with directors who ask actors to create their own blocking, student actors should learn how to block a scene.

To block a scene, the actor needs to decide where the scene is taking place. The actor needs to think like a scene designer and establish what scenic elements would be on stage if the actor were performing the scene in a fully realized play production. The actor needs to imagine that they are performing the scene in such a production with an adequate budget. What would the set include? What would it look like? The actor should identify entrances and exits, the placement of doors, windows, furniture, props, and all other needed scenic elements.

Once the actor has established the setting, the actor should make a drawing of it. For this class and others like it, the actor can take a standard sheet of notebook paper and turn it on its side, with the part of the page nearest the actor as downstage, the part to the actor's left facing the page being stage right, the upper portion of the paper being upstage, and the right side of the paper as stage left. The actor can draw a rectangle within the sheet to represent the stage playing area. Within the playing area, the actor can do a rough, thumbnail sketch, not to scale, of the setting that identifies the location of all scenic elements. This can also be done with electronic devices, but by the time I type this sentence, whatever software I reference will be obsolete, so let us just stick with the dinosaur tactic of pencil and paper.

Once the actor has created the sketch, they can make whatever adjustments are needed to fit the setting into the rehearsal location. In the case of this class, the actor can imagine that the class is in a three-quarter thrust playing space. The center of the classroom will be emptied as the class pushes all desks and chairs to the walls. The class arranges the chairs along the north, east, and south walls, keeping the west wall as a backstage space. The downstage area will be the east wall, so when the class faces east, they are facing downstage. The north wall is stage left, the south wall is stage right, and the west wall is upstage. When the class rehearses and performs, students will sit in the stage left, stage right, and downstage areas of the space, so when blocking and playing their scene, actors can keep in mind the audience sight lines of all three sides of the "house." In "house" speak, the audience will be sitting house right, house left, and house center.

Once the actor has established the setting and has a sketch to record it, the next decision is to establish the starting point for all actors in the scene. The following instructions correlate to a two-person scene. Where are the characters sitting or standing when they say their first lines? The actors can search for clues or references in the scene's script. If there are no clues, the actors should read the rest of the script to see what the characters were doing in the actual moments before their scene. The moment before is what happened in the lives of the characters preceding this onstage event that caused them to be in the scene, doing what they are doing. If this information is not available in the scene and for some reason the actors cannot read the full script, then the actors need to use their own imaginations and extrapolate the moment before and choose a physical starting position for the scene.

At this point I will address the elephant in the room: as an actor in an acting class, you may be saying to yourself, "Self, why do we even need blocking, can we not just sit and talk to each other?" Sitting and talking for the whole scene is a choice. I ask, though: is it the strongest choice? In the art of theatre, audiences come to see a play, not just to hear it. Theatre is a performance art that, like dance, requires movement. Acting for the stage is different from acting for the camera.

It is recommended that students in this class incorporate blocking into their scene work. Look for imaginative opportunities to illustrate the dramatic action of the dialogue through movement, composition, and picturization. Movement, composition, and picturization are covered in much greater detail in Acting II and Directing I. You should take those classes.

Legally Blonde

You may say to yourself, "Self, just sitting and talking works in movies and television. There are electronic forms of acting that succeed as merely talking heads entertainment." True, but in a television sitcom, for instance, while the actor sits in one spot, the camera does not. The camera angle changes often, either by moving the camera or by cutting to a different camera. The camera viewpoint changes often. Take a situation comedy like *The Conners* or *Mom,* or even classics like *Friends* or *Seinfeld,* where the scenes are filmed before a live studio audience. There are several cameras set up to film the action, usually about four. Every few seconds, the picture will cut to that of a different camera. This gives the illusion of movement and blocking, even when the characters are sitting in a booth drinking coffee, as in many a *Seinfeld* episode.

In movies they accomplish the same effect, even when only filming with one camera. They film the same scene several times with the camera in a different spot each time. Then, in the editing process, they cut from camera point to camera point in order to create viewpoint changes. This gives the illusion of blocking for scenes where characters sit in one spot and talk to each other. While movies and television give the illusion of blocking, on stage, actors use actual blocking.

There are, of course, exceptions to every rule. There may be stage plays with scenes designed and intended to be static, with no motion or blocking. Who says that in those scenes the two characters just sit and talk? If the stage directions say that the characters sit at a restaurant table, who wrote those stage directions? If they came from the playwright, the playwright is not the director of the scene. The job of staging the scene is that of a director, and since students in this class are not working with a director, it becomes each student's job. Other than what to say, students should not let the playwright tell them how to do their jobs. The student actor, serving as their own director, should decide if there are movement opportunities when staging the scene.

When I was an undergraduate taking a directing class, the professor instructed us to take a black marker to our scripts and eradicate all stage directions. One reason was because they might be the record of the initial director's blocking, and if so, we would be copying that director's work rather than creating our own.

In this class, it is the actors who stage the scenes with the aid of their professor. Theatre is a collaborative art form and the playwright is only one of the many team members. The opinion of the student actor is just as valid as that of the playwright when it comes to staging the scene. Across time and space, the playwright is suggesting blocking to the actors; however, the playwright, without a time machine, can have no idea about where you are performing the scene and the capabilities of your performance space. The blocking the playwrights describe may have looked great in their heads, but they could not possibly predict how it will look or play in our classroom. In the final analysis, the playwright's stage directions are only suggestions, not commands.

Now that the elephant has been dealt with and the need for actors to block scenes in this class has been determined, here are the basics for actors to consider when blocking their scenes. Actors should do a script analysis of the scene in order to identify the action verbs the writer has

Legally Blonde

selected for the dialogue. In a good script—assume the chosen selection is good until proven otherwise—each word has been carefully selected by the writer as the best word for that moment in the play's action. An analysis of the action verbs may help the actor identify the spurs to action hidden in the dialogue. The concept of spurs was discussed in detail in Chapter 8. If necessary, go back and review that information.

In brief, a spur is a word in the script that goads, impels, or urges the character to an illustrative and relevant physical action. These shifts in thought or emotion, a desire to be close or to move away, a sign of vulnerability or increased defense, are opportunities for the actor to create physical actions that are natural, seemingly spontaneous, and free. The same principle applies here for scene work as it did in Chapter 8 on the body and movement in monologues. Blocking should illustrate the underlying dramatic action of the scene, what is going on between the two characters as they say the dialogue. An audience should be able to tell what is transpiring even without verbalization, like a silent movie or a stage pantomime.

That sounds good, right? But when I first learned this concept, my reaction was to ask, "How the heck am I supposed to do that?" Actors can accomplish this by analyzing the action verbs in the script and using them as inspiration for physical movement in the stage space. For example, look at this sequence from my play, *Victimology*. It is the first page of the script and the audience is seeing these characters for the first time. The scene is set in a barn.

(1) VERN
So the salesman **walks up** to the farmer and says excuse me, where do I **sit**?

(2) TED
The salesman says that?

(3) VERN
No, I said that. Where do I **sit**?

(4) TED
Pull up a chair, bale of hay, anything.

(5) VERN
Reminds me of home. I was **raised** in a barn, y'know. The salesman, anyway, he says to the farmer, "My car **broke down**. Can I **sleep** here tonight?" Farmer says, "Yup, but you'll have to **sleep with** the red-headed school teacher." Salesman **lights up** with a big old grin see and he goes, "Fine. And I **assure** you, sir, I am a perfect gentleman." "Good," says the farmer. "So's he." I **love** that joke. What's your favorite joke?

(6) TED
You won't **like** it.

(7) VERN
Come on, come on, I **drank** enough beer I'll **laugh** at anything.

The scene begins with the two characters walking onto the set. For the sake of this example, say they enter from stage right. In the first line, Vern uses the verbs "walks up" and "sit." The actor playing this line can use the first verb as a spur to cross stage left and look for a place to sit down as they go, and for stage business once the cross is complete. Vern repeats the verb "sit" in the third line. The actor has a choice: this repeated verb can inspire the actor to move about the space, continuing the search for seating, or the actor can stand motionless, emphasizing that the other character has failed to meet their demands. Ted responds in Line 4 by instructing Vern to "pull up" his choice of seating.

The instruction to "pull up" implies that the majority of the stage floor is empty. Perhaps all the seating possibilities, such as bales of hay, sawhorses, and chairs, are all pushed against the walls of the barn. The actor playing Ted may use this verb as inspiration to give an impromptu tour of the space, pointing out the seating choices for Vern. Ted can also demonstrate or gesture to Vern their instructions for Vern to not only choose a piece of seating, but to drag it, perhaps to center stage. Maybe Ted leads by example and drags a chair or bale of hay to center stage and indicates that Vern should reciprocate and join Ted there.

In the next line, Vern says "raised," "broke down," "sleep," "sleep with," and "lights up," associated with the facial expression of grinning, then "assure" and "love." These are all good action verbs for blocking spurs. "Raised" might spur Vern to look the barn up and down, perhaps crossing up stage and down stage, or side to side in order to give the space a good inspection. "Broke down," "sleep," and the partially repetitive "sleep with" are indications of vulnerability, so to seek intimacy with Ted, Vern might close the distance between them. This would be logical as Vern is telling a dirty joke, so intimacy indicative of a sex act would be desired, especially as the joke in question hinges on physical intimacy. Perhaps not only does Vern get near Ted, but if Ted is sitting, Vern also lowers his body to a sitting position so that Ted and Vern are on the same level. Then, with "lights up" Vern might be spurred to stand up tall, step away, and spread his arms wide, illustrating the concept of elevated spirits and enthusiasm.

"Assure" might spur Vern to a return to intimacy; perhaps he crosses to stage right of Ted and puts his left arm across Ted's shoulder. The use of the verb "love" comes after the joke's punch line. Perhaps Vern will use it as a spur to decrease intimacy and move away. Perhaps Vern, who later reveals that he identifies as heterosexual, needs to prove his sexual orientation by moving away from Ted, showing a disinterest in sex between two men.

Ted might pick up on a desire for distance as expressed by Vern and cross even farther away when he vocalizes the action verb "like." Both men have at this point crossed away from each other, putting a vast distance between themselves. This can serve to illustrate Ted's defensiveness about the nature of his sense of humor. These men are unalike, especially in terms of humor, and Ted crossing farther away from Vern illustrates this variation.

The sequence ends with Vern's use of the verbs "drank" and "laugh" in response to Ted's erection of a defensive wall. This effort to remove the wall might spur Vern to cut the distance between the two men. If Vern is stage left and Ted is stage right, perhaps Vern halves the distance between them by crossing to center stage. Drinking together, as they have been doing in the moments before the play begins, implies intimacy. They are drinking buddies. The verb "laugh" is also meant as an encouragement for Ted to tell his joke and might inspire Vern, through body language and gestures, to communicate positive energy to his uncertain and anxious friend. These are some suggestions for how this exchange between these two characters might be blocked. Identifying and analyzing the action verbs helps actors draw a road map for playing the scene. Students in this class can use this process to schematize a blocking pattern for scenes.

Identifying the action spurs in dialogue is one way to figure out how to block a scene. The next way involves a process called *verbing*. Verbing assumes that each line of dialogue in the script is not a line of dialogue but an action the speaking character is taking upon the listening character. The line of dialogue is the symbol of an action. These actions, when put together, serve as a key to illustrating the scene through physical movement. A line of dialogue means an instance of speaking for the character as designated in the script. A line of dialogue can be one word, one sentence, several sentences, or a monologue. It is when the character begins to speak until they finish, and another character responds by speaking.

The way to verb a line is to determine the line's aim, what it is the speaker is doing to the other character by talking. The action verb should either end with an "s," as in, "She hammers him with this line," or an "ing," as in, "She is hammering him with this line." The "s" ending is a stronger choice as it is more immersive and immediate; "ing" places a layer of distance, as though the actor is observing the action rather than partaking in it.

One example that shows that choices do not have to be literal involves an actor saying the line, "I love you! I love you! Love! Love! Love!" Perhaps the character's action needs to show the character's desperate need to convince the listener that their love is true. Their goal is to convince their partner of their love's veracity. Perhaps the character needs to show artless earnestness? What creature that humans encounter on a regular basis demonstrates unconditional love with artless exuberance? Dogs; therefore, one choice of an action for the actor to perform the line would be, "They bark." Playing the action of barking, "I love you! I love you! Love!

Legally Blonde

Love! Love!" would give the actor ideas on movements to illustrate barking. They could incorporate canine characteristics into their body language, facial expressions, and movement pattern.

Another possibility could be coupled with the line, "I hate you so much, I really do," as Sally says to Harry near the end of *When Harry Met Sally*. In this case, perhaps the actor wants to play the opposite and say the line in a way that conveys the opposite of enmity. If the actor verbs the line with the action verb of "stroke," as in "She strokes him," that will greatly metamorphose the vocal delivery, as well as suggest facial expressions, gestures, and blocking patterns. A placid face, a gentle, smooth petting motion of the hands, coupled with a cross to the listening character for intimacy, or perhaps the speaker strokes the cheek of the listener while delivering the line: all these ideas could be borne by identifying the underlying verb of the line as "strokes" or "stroking."

A final example can be applied to one of the most famous lines of the stage, a line that has arguably been delivered in every possible fashion: "To be, or not to be, that is the question." Who is Hamlet's scene partner? God, or the audience in direct address. The actor can pick one. What is Hamlet's goal? To justify his choice to die is one possible choice for an actor. Hamlet is depressed, wracked with grief, and talks often of suicide, so what if his desire to die is genuine and he is galvanizing himself in order to take the leap? To persuade God or the audience that his choice of self-slaughter is a good one, he might choose one of two tactics: he might seduce, by being nice, or he might induce, by being nasty. Let us imagine he chooses to threaten rather than cajole. In such a case, we might verb the line with "hammering" as in, "He hammers." The choice of hammering then can infuse every aspect of the actor's performance choices, especially gesturing and blocking. A strong choice would be for the actor to cross emphatically from upstage to downstage to a spot downstage center. This is one of the strongest movements a character can make, and if the point of address chosen by the actor includes audience direct address, this movement towards the "other" in the scene is a powerfully strong illustrative choice. Hamlet is overcoming objections through sheer force before they can even be offered.

Identifying spurs and verbing lines can both conjure blocking. A third resource comes from analyzing the dramatic action in the scene and then illustrating it through movement. This is similar to verbing, but on a larger scale. By compiling the verbing phrases into a linear list, an actor can use that list to create this dramatic action analysis.

First the actor identifies the character's scene goal. Referencing from an earlier chapter how a character's superobjective for the play works: each beat has an aim, and all of those aims lead inexorably to the accomplishment of the scene's goal. Each scene has a goal, and all these goals lead to the accomplishment of the act's objective. Each act, the character has an objective, and these objectives should lead to the accomplishment of the play's superobjective. The actor in this class trying to create blocking must decide their character's scene goal. It should result from all the character's actions in each line and every beat that constitutes the scene.

Once the actor has determined the character's scene goal, the actor surmises what might be some physical actions the character might take to achieve that goal. The actor can use those physical actions to inspire blocking design. Imagine that you are playing a character whose goal in a scene section is to pursue, or capture, their scene partner. If your character is pursuing the other character, perhaps by questioning them or debating them, and the other character is being evasive, perhaps by providing unsatisfying answers, avoiding questions, or by refusing to budge on a point of opinion, then you and your partner might illustrate that action through your blocking. Your character can physically chase the other character around the set. The interrogator character poses a question. The other character, as they answer or refuse to answer, moves to another section of the stage. The interrogator character, on their next line, follows them. This pattern can continue until there is a change in the dramatic action.

Imagine two characters in a scene are arguing—a literal debate is occurring between them, so actors could illustrate their verbal combat with moves akin to a boxing match. Perhaps during relaxed moments, they retreat to a set corner; perhaps during intense moments, they meet in the set's center, like boxers meeting in the center of the ring. Perhaps they circle each other, looking for an opening or a weakness in the other's argument. Another possibility could be to have the blocking suggest a game of chess, or checkers. The idea is that the actors choose an active form of conflict, such as a sport or game, and then use movements associated with that form of conflict as a basis for creating blocking.

Another tactic actors can use to inform their blocking choices is to illustrate the relationship between the characters through the use of proximity. When the characters are warm to each other, in agreement, they might relax and sit close to one another. In moments of disagreement or strife, they might stand and move away from each other. This and the other tactics we have discussed to this point are ways actors can use script analysis to assess the dramatic action sequences in a scene, and then use these aims, goals, and actions to create blocking informed by the dialogue that illustrates the action and supports the characters' intentions. This creates organic, natural, and powerful blocking that communicates the scene to the audience consciously and subconsciously through non-verbal methods.

Once students have imagined a blocking plan, it needs to be recorded. The mechanics and methods of doing that deed can vary, but procedures proposed below, if used, require the following materials:

1. Floor plan sketch
2. Actor tokens
3. Paper copies of the script for both actors
4. Pencils and erasers
5. Two different colored highlighters

Exercise 1: Blocking

Step 1
Actors should take their sketch of the floor plan and put it on a desk or table so that the acting team can work on it together.

Step 2
Actors should decide on a starting location for their characters. Actors can take tokens that represent each of them—perhaps coins labeled to identify which coin represents one actor and which represents the other—and set them on the starting points on the floor plan. Coins are recommended because they slide across the paper relatively easily, but character tokens can be anything small in stature, like Monopoly game player pieces. Of the original Monopoly set, I prefer the Boot or the Race Car, but each to their own. Labeled coins are better, though, because then actors do not have to worry about forgetting which token represents whom.

Step 3
As the acting team goes through the scene, they can try out the blocking by moving their tokens around the floor plan. If both actors agree that certain blocking works, they need to record it. The acting team can write the blocking down on the script in pencil. It is not necessary to write out full words. Actors can abbreviate, thusly:

X = cross	DS = downstage	DSC = downstage center
SR = stage right	SL = stage left	C = center stage
U = upstage	UL = upstage left	UR = upstage right

For areas in between, actors can use symbols like XSRC, which means somewhere between SR and C, like halfway between center and stage right. Actors should use these as a test kitchen for coming up with their own blocking shorthand. The idea is to write as few letters as possible to remind the actors what the blocking is for that moment in the scene. It is the need to write things down quickly and easily that leads to the use of paper scripts, pencils, and erasers in this class; the pencils and erasers are because the blocking might change or evolve as acting teams rehearse their scenes.

Step 4
Once students have a blocking plan, they can test it by putting the scene on its feet. To do this, they can clear a rehearsal space, then put representations of furniture, like chairs, tables, or rehearsal blocks, in place to approximate the furniture of the floor plan. Students can rehearse the scene, and as

Lesson 22—Blocking a Scene   183

needed, adjust the blocking. If this is done, students should be sure to erase the old blocking and write in the new blocking.

1. Student teams should record their blocking on both scripts so that they have a complete record of the scene entire, including dialogue and a whole movement plan for both characters. This way if one partner shows up at rehearsal having forgotten their script, the team can still hold an effective rehearsal.
2. This is also helpful in case one partner misremembers things. If the two partners decide on a blocking pattern, then the next rehearsal one partner does something different, the team has a record of the agreed-upon blocking and can get back on track. It is hoped that all acting partners are great, but one cannot count on that being the case, so all students need to protect themselves from the potential incompetence of others.

Step 5

This step is intended to further cement the blocking scheme in the students' memories. Once acting teams have agreed upon blocking that has been tested on its feet with actual run-throughs, they should take their floor plan sketch and diagram the blocking on the floor plan. One actor can use one colored highlighter to identify them, and a second color to identify the other partner.

1. Identify the starting points for each character by drawing a small circle with the character's initials in it at its starting point. Write the number "1" next to the circles to show that these are the characters' first positions.
2. When the character moves, draw a series of arrows that form a line in the direction the character crosses to its second position. Write the number "2" next to this location of the initialed circle representing the character so that the acting team knows this is the characters' second position.
3. Use the highlighter to trace along the arrows' paths and to fill in each initialed circle to record the characters' movements.

One floor plan sketch should be enough for a short scene, but if it gets too convoluted, the acting team can make a second copy of the floor plan and continue to diagram movements on it and subsequent copies as needed. This will create a complete pictorial almanac, a road map of the blocking for the scene.

Step 6

Rehearse, rehearse, rehearse. There are four general rules to good acting and being physically adept at a scene's required movements is third on the list. The list for actors is as follows:

1. Show up on time.
2. Know your lines.
3. Do not bump into the furniture.
4. Be nice to people.

The best way to learn is to do. The more often student actors create blocking by going through the process described in this chapter, the better students will become at bringing the script's physical aspects to life. Even if the blocking scheme for this class does not work, is deemed weak by classmates or professors, or suffers from some other inequity, students will have learned by doing it. Students will learn movement concepts that are successful or movement concepts that are fiascoes, but the paramount component is that students learned, and in so doing improved their future endeavors. By this claim, the blocking students devise for their second scene will be better than the blocking for this first scene.

Exercise 2

1. Students: get with your scene partner. Create a blocking scheme for the team's Scene #1. Write out the blocking on each team member's script so that both actors have a complete copy of the blocking plan. Do this while sitting together at a desk with a sketch of the team floor plan. This exercise is timed for thirty minutes.

2. Once all teams have a blocking scheme, the class will start putting scenes on their feet and testing their efficacy. Each team will run their scene before the class and receive feedback as to whether adjustments are needed.

3. Once blocking is evaluated and finalized, student teams should take three copies of the scene's floor plan and create three copies of the color-coded blocking diagram; this gives one copy to each actor and one copy to the professor, who will keep that copy as part of the class record. Failure to produce these copies will have a negative impact on the student team's performance grade. This blocking diagram should be turned into the professor the next class after the team's blocking has been evaluated and finalized. If the class gets to a team today, the blocking diagram will be due next class.

4. Student teams should get to work now. Thirty minutes and the class will begin putting scenes on feet.

Lesson 23
Repetition and the Illusion of the First Time
Band Name or Chapter Title?

When it comes to acting, actors are all mad scientists. Actors are Dr. Frankenstein, the performance is the monster, and they run around it yelling, "It's alive! It's alive!" That is the dream, anyway; all actors want their performances to appear alive and fresh to the audience, which can be a challenge. For the audience, the performance is a new experience. For the fictional characters in the scene or play, this is a new experience; they have never performed these actions or said these words. But for the actors playing the scene or play, this is a repeat of material they have gone over possibly hundreds of times.

When all the readings of the scene during the analysis phase are taken into account, coupled with the innumerable repetitions required during the memorization process, then all of the readings during rehearsals, and the run-throughs once the actors are off-book are added, it amounts to repetition on an epic scale. By the time actors rehearsing a play are ready for an audience, they know the material better than the writer. The actor becomes so familiar with the material that they run the risk of breeding contempt through familiarity. The relationship between script and actor is intimate.

And student actors in this class are only preparing for one performance! Professional actors often commit to long contracts and hundreds of performances. Terrence Mann, while running a workshop in his video *Auditions and Insights,* describes what he calls "longrunitis," which he encountered in his over one thousand-performance run in *Cats* on Broadway. I have never faced such a lengthy challenge, but in the summer of 1992, I was in the cast of *The Legend of Daniel Boone,* an outdoor historical drama in Harrodsburg, Kentucky. We ran six shows a week for three months. By the end of the season, I had fallen in and out of love with the show, but audience number eighty-nine deserved the same enthusiastic performance as that received by the opening night audience.

The actor's problem is that, while the actor is intimately familiar with the material, the character is not, and this newness to the character is called the illusion of the first time. A primary task of the actor is to create this illusion in every repetition, be it a rehearsal or a performance. The most difficult aspect of this duality is that the character does not know how the scene ends; for the character, fate is open-ended. The actor knows how everything goes, but they must purport that they do not.

Actors repetitively doing a scene run the risk of losing their energy, liveliness, and spontaneity. This chapter will identify ways in which an actor can meet the challenge of averting these perilous tendencies. Actors can try varying the performance, evolving the performance, having faith in imagination, and intensifying their focus on the moment.

The first way to keep the illusion of the first time is by making every repetition not an exact repetition. If an actor does it slightly differently each time, they are performing something new and not actually repeating anything. To be clear, you must realize that no one can ever exactly repeat a performance. Human beings are not robots, and so can never repeat physical actions and verbalizations with machine accuracy. Actors in live performance, unlike an old VCR, cannot be rewound so the scene can be replayed. The scene will subconsciously be a little different each time. To keep a performance fresh, actors focus on conscious differences, and do something a little different each time. Whether it be line delivery, gestures, blocking, or stage business, variety is the spice of life—and the stage.

The Great Gatsby

With line delivery, actors can vary things up by picking a different word in a sentence or sentences to emphasize. Most syllable emphases are set by the proper pronunciation of the word, but often putting an emphasis on one word or another can subtly or greatly change the meaning of a line. Either consciously or unconsciously, actors make choices in some sentences as to which word or words they will emphasize when speaking the line.

Exercise 1: Word Emphasis

1. Actors should go over their lines as they perform them now and identify which words, if any, they are saying with special emphasis.
2. Lightly mark these words with pencil underlining.
3. After this, actors should go back and identify alternate words for possible emphasis. Erase the old pencil underlining and underline these new choices.
4. Try the lines with the new emphases choices and assess their value to the playing of the scene.

While the above is a good exercise, acting students do not need to be so formal about it. Once actors are off-book, they can just experiment with emphasis, and if something works, they can remember it for possible use. If something does not work, they can discard it and abandon it resolutely.

In addition to variations in word emphasis, the actor can also experiment with line delivery technique, especially volume, pitch, tone, and quality. Actors should go back over their lines while paying attention to how they usually say them. This promotes vocal variety. One thing that can suck life out of line delivery is staying too much in the middle, in this case as it relates to volume. In life, people do not maintain monotonous volume; they get louder and quieter regularly when they speak for various reasons. Acting students should be sure to vary their volume. The acting student should alternate sections of loud, quiet, and mid-range in order to try new things that keep repeat performances fresh.

Exercise 2: Vocal Variety

1. Actors need to go over their lines as they perform them now, paying attention to where in every line they are loud, where they are quiet, and where their volume is in the middle range.
2. Actors should go over their lines as they usually say them, making note of the pitch of their voice. Be aware of the use of low tones, middle-range tones, and high tones. At what parts of the speech does the actor use their bass and soprano voice, or do they leave it all in the middle? Do not leave it all in the middle. Once actors have identified opportunities for exploring the expressiveness of their vocal range in speaking, much like

how singers use their vocal range when singing, they can look for ways to vary usage to keep repeat performances fresh and new.

3. Actors should go over lines as they usually say them and listen to their vocal tone usage. Pamelia S. Phillips describes tone in an article titled "Defining Tone in Singing": "*Tone* is known as the *color* or *timbre* of your singing voice. Every voice has a specific color, which can best be described as warm, dark, or strident." The same is true for actors speaking lines in that some areas of the line may be spoken with affection, others with sadness, still others with anger. It is the sound of the voice conveying how the character feels about the words that they are saying. The actor can identify the emotional connotations they have endowed on the various words or phrases in their lines, the color-coding of their lines per emotional symbology, which is discussed in a previous chapter. Once identified, the actor can attempt to make changes in subsequent deliveries to spawn fresh ways to speak the lines.

4. Actors should go over their lines as they are accustomed to while scrutinizing their vocal quality use. Vocal quality includes descriptions like smooth, raspy, whispered, breathy, shaky, and full-voiced. Once actors have identified the application of different qualities to vocalizations, they can go back and consider changes. Try these changes in ensuing performances as a way of keeping them crisp and fresh.

Gestures can also generate the illusion of the first time in repeat performances. Actors can go through their scene while paying attention to their use of gestures, firming up their grasp on what they are doing with their hands in order to communicate the script's meaning to the audience and their intentions to their scene partner. It may be that the actor has carefully choreographed the use of their hands, as they are a powerful acting tool and the actor should always understand and intend what they are saying with their hands. A good plan is to work out specifics but also improvise and vary things in order to keep the performance from being stale and losing meaning. Actors do not fall into ruts with gesture work. Try different gestures; perhaps better ones will be found. In any event, trying different gestures from performance to performance, whether they are big changes or small and nuanced, is a way to keep repeat performances from stagnating.

While actors may try big changes in gesturing, it is not recommended that they make big changes in blocking. An actor can try small variations within the larger pattern. If the blocking calls for an actor to cross and sit on the sofa, maybe they can try a slightly different approach to the sofa or sit down in a slightly different way. If the sitting location on the sofa is not pre-determined or germane, perhaps they can try sitting on a different portion of the sofa. If the blocking pattern calls for the actor to cross from center stage to stage right, perhaps they take a different path by putting a slight upstage or downstage arc to the cross. Perhaps the actor takes a slightly more upstage path than normal, going past their mark, then turning to face stage left and coming back to their mark from the other side. These are ways actors can change small blocking details without changing the inherent pattern.

The Great Gatsby

Actors do not want to overly change the blocking because this is the blocking pattern the acting partners agreed upon. It is possible, through rehearsal, to discover new ideas and make changes to the blocking that could improve it. This is true of all artistic endeavors. But at some point, acting partners need to say that the scene is set, which means no large changes can be made, this is the way the team needs to rehearse the scene. Once the team agrees that the scene is set, there should be no large changes to the blocking, especially changes that one partner tries out without advance warning to the other partner. Making large changes to the blocking may throw off one's partner and the scene. This kind of rogue behavior can serve to create friction between partners. Resentment might blossom towards an actor who changes things without warning a partner, even as the partner who made the change might resent the other partner for crushing their freewheeling artistry. The best solution, if an actor intends to identify small alterations to blocking as a way of keeping performances fresh, is to make small changes within the larger blocking scheme so that the blocking still fits the original, agreed upon final plan.

Stage business, on the other hand, is the actor's private purview and is solely up to the individual actor. The actor can try different physical activities every performance if they remember that the purpose of stage business is to add relevant dimension to the character's personality. Stage business cannot be random activity. If the character is tired, perhaps in the moments when they are listening they close their eyes and nod their head. If the character is nervous, perhaps they chew a fingernail or repeatedly run their fingers through their hair. The stage business needs to grow logically from the character's identity and not distract from the scene. The scene remains about its subject, which the actor derived from analysis, not about what the actor's body is doing while listening and speaking. Using one of the above examples, do not turn a scene from *A Doll's House* into a scene about nail-biting and hair care. With these restrictions in mind, stage business is an incredibly rich vein that actors can explore to keep each performance fresh and new. If an actor discovers some bit of stage business that is especially effective, the actor can make it part of the permanent scene movement scheme.

Another way for actors to keep performances alive is line delivery, or line interpretation. Some people are good at cold readings. Often in cold-reading auditions, actors find excellent line readings. Sometimes their delivery of some lines never evolves from the cold-reading audition to opening night. Does that mean their performance is stale and staid? Even if actors think they have the perfect delivery for a certain line, they should not settle for that line interpretation; rehearsal and repeat performances offer opportunities for experimentation.

Actors need to continue searching for other possible meanings to the line. An actor may have decided that they know exactly what the character means when they say a line, but what if the character actually means something else? Perhaps the actor used analysis, the mind's logical detective skills, to determine the line's meaning. What if they approached it from the soul instead, and examined the line from the emotional point of view instead of cold logic? Gene Wilder discusses this when he talks about the improvisatory scene work he did with Richard Pryor in the film *Silver Streak*. "I don't say that Richard's way is without any thought—but his method always has an emotional, rather than an intellectual, base. In this regard, Richard was my teacher: no thinking—just immediate, instinctive response. If it's no good, the director will cut it out—assuming you have a director who wants you to improvise" (Wilder 2005, 164–165). Actors can examine each line's emotional range and try new things.

In an analysis, an actor may have decided what the aims and goals are for their character in the beats and the overall scene. Is that analysis per-

Lesson 23—Repetition and the Illusion of the First Time

The Great Gatsby

fect? What if the actor varied those up? The actor does not need to discuss these things with their partner because they are the actor's private parts of their play acting. Their partner should respond to the actor no matter what the actor gives their partner. In that classic dinner scene I imagined earlier in this book to illustrate action beats, a character wanted the mashed potatoes from the grandparent. Imagine that you are the actor playing that part, and that is the aim that you settled on. What if you changed that aim? What if, instead of wanting the potatoes for yourself, you wanted to keep your grandparent from eating the potatoes because the starch will metabolize and add to their sugar level, causing their diabetes to strike them dead? Changing aims, goals, and motives are experiments that can lead to fresh new performances.

Actors can also continue to search for other possible spurs, triggers, and verbings for lines. Maybe the verb an actor settled on for a line is good, but they can try different verbs and maybe even find a better one. Each different verb, since the actor is performing that verb's action when they say the line, will bring new line delivery. Changing the spurs and triggers will change how the character listens, how and when the character reacts to the other character while they speak. Some actors, even some articles on acting and book titles, insist that "acting is reacting." If so, changing what a character does while they listen to another character, how the character reacts to what the other character says and does, is another great technique for exploring how to keep a performance fresh. By the way, "Acting is Reacting" is the title of an article written by Dan W. Mullin and published in *The Tulane Drama Review*, Vol. 5, No. 3, March 1961. This is a great article that I first encountered while in graduate school at Florida State University and its title has stuck with me ever since.

To keep repeat performances of a scene gleaming and glittering, either in rehearsal or a long run, actors use their imaginations. Actors never quit thinking, fantasizing, and reconnoitering about the scene. Actors concentrate on the imaginary details and this keeps them in the moment rather than thinking about what just happened or trying to control what will happen next. Sidney Poitier says that the secret to good acting is realizing cause and effect. Acting at its best is reacting to stimuli (acting is reacting), as people spend most of their lives doing just that. He has this to say about how actors and audiences experience life:

> I'm broadened as an actor the moment I realize that when people sit in a theater and watch me expressing feelings similar to their own, they can tell if I'm really experiencing those emotions or if I'm faking them . . . they know whether I'm interpreting them in a genuine way or just play-acting. Living consciously involves being genuine; it involves listening and responding to others honestly and openly; it involves being in the moment. This is all equally true of effective acting. Acting isn't a game of "pretend." It's an exercise in being real. (Poitier 2000, 145–147)

I get where he is coming from, but this is where the confusion with the method actor's acting theories comes from. He says do not pretend, rather be real, and because everything is cause and effect, all an actor does is honestly react to stimuli. But what if it is seventy-eight degrees in the theatre but for the character the temperature is twenty degrees below zero? What if the actor is on a wooden stage and the character is on a sandy beach? How then can the actor's honest reactions, free from pretense, serve the performance? They cannot. Actors do have to pretend. What Poitier means is that actors engage their imagination with the play's given circumstances to a degree that they become real to the character. Actors pretend so intensely that for the character part of them, fantasy becomes reality. And by fully imagining the fantasy reality, actors create the effects that give their character cause.

Good acting in a scene comes from focusing on the moment. Gene Wilder (2005) agrees:

> . . . and, try to stay in the moment, which only means that every time you do the same scene, on stage or in front of a camera, if you're relaxed and you're reacting to the other actors at that moment—not the way you did it yesterday or fifteen minutes ago—then even though the lines are exactly the same and the staging is exactly the same, the scene will be a little different each time you do it, and it will be alive. (82)

Lesson 23—Repetition and the Illusion of the First Time

Actors should be clear on what their aims are. They need to know what it is that their character wants. Actors need to be clear on what their tactics are, know how they plan to achieve their aims. Actors should try to have a genuine impact on their acting partner and say the line truthfully while playing the underlying action. The character is trying to do something to the other character, so actors should force their partners to respond to them by having a genuine impact on them. An actor should not let a partner ignore them or play the scene repetitiously.

The Great Gatsby

Even though the actor knows the outcome of the scene, they should try to change the outcome, especially if it does not go their character's way. Actors need to believe that anything is possible, that if they play hard and true enough that their character will succeed even if the script says that they will fail. Even in the saddest tragedy, the character believes they will achieve their superobjective until the moment they fail. The tragic play *Romeo and Juliet* is a comedy until Romeo kills Tybalt. Juliet sees that as an obstacle to being with Romeo, but still believes in their happily ever after until Juliet sees Romeo's corpse. Then Juliet gives up. But not until that moment, and the actor playing Juliet must also believe until that selfsame moment.

It is a total Yoda thing, from *The Empire Strikes Back*: "Do or do not. There is no try." So in a way, actor training is the same as Jedi training. And that's pretty cool.

Exercise 3: Winning

I first encountered Robert Cohen's book, *Acting One*, as a doctoral student in an acting theory class at Florida State University. One of the exercises he crafted had such an impact on me, it has stayed with me for all these years and inspired my creation of the following exercise. His exercise is called "Resonating," and in it Cohen (2008) directs student actors to use the power of vibrations created by the human voice to accomplish certain tasks. It reminded me of the Marvel Comics characters Black Bolt from *Inhumans* and Banshee from *X-Men*. Yes, I am a comic book nerd. Anyway, here's my exercise, which I call "Winning: Expecting Victory."

1. Students: find a section of wall, window, or floor. Stand near it.
2. Students, using only your voice, make the wall move.
   A. Realize that the wall is made up of atoms and that they are subject to the laws of physics. Realize that sound is vibration. Realize that your voice is sound. Realize that your voice is made up of vibrations. Realize that the wall is affected by vibrations.
   B. Now, make the wall move again, or vibrate, only with your voice, while believing you can make the wall move.
3. Students choose a partner.
4. One member of the team, using only their voice, needs to make their partner move.
   A. Students: realize that your partner's body is no different than the wall, window, or floor. Realize that the power of your voice can do to your partner's body what it did to the wall, window, or floor.
   B. Believing that you can, now make your partner's body move using only your voice.

Exercise 4: Brainstorming

1. Students, think to yourself: what are some things in life that you cannot explain, that defy belief, that seem otherworldly, magical, or impossible, but somehow exist?
   A. The professor can poll the class, and as students respond, list responses on the white board or other writing tool.
   B. The class can now discuss items on the list as proof that things exist that we are taught are impossible.
      a. Students need to use these possible impossibilities as a basis for the Warlock Wizard Wand Battle Exercise: partners face off in a magic battle using wands to cast spells and defend against them. Students need to believe in the magic.
      b. Telekinesis Battle Exercise: partners are characters who can use their minds to move things. Students need to battle each other like telekinetic sumo wrestlers.

Lesson 24
Scene #1 Rehearsal

Rehearsal day for Scene #1, the serious or tragic scene. The professor will design a rehearsal for this class and the entire class will be spent with partners rehearsing their scenes with each other for the entire period.

Lesson 25
Day Two
Scene #1 Rehearsal

The class will rehearse Scene #1 off-book. Actors may still call for line, which means each team will need to partner with another team, so that someone is on book for everyone. Those not on book need to pay close attention to each scene, take notes, and offer feedback when requested or appropriate.

Lesson 26
Day Three
Scene #1 Rehearsal

This is the final dress rehearsal for Scene #1.

It is not recommended that actors call for line, but if an actor absolutely cannot get through the scene, then the actor may call for line. Best results will come if student actors treat today like a performance rather than a rehearsal.

Acting I Scene #1 Evaluation

Name _____   Score _____

Character Focus
1   2   3   4   5   6   7   8   9   10

Emotion Action
1   2   3   4   5   6   7   8   9   10

Partner Communication
1   2   3   4   5   6   7   8   9   10

Energy
1   2   3   4   5   6   7   8   9   10

Blocking Performance
1   2   3   4   5   6   7   8   9   10

Body Language
1   2   3   4   5   6   7   8   9   10

Comments:

Lesson 27
Scene #1 Performance

1. The professor will call for teams to perform in the order determined by the professor.
2. Once a team is called, they should set up furniture and props as needed for their performance. Once the performance space is ready, the team will wait for the professor to tell them to begin.
3. For opening slate, actors should say their names, as in Actor One says, "Hi, I'm Bilbo Baggins," then Actor Two follows with "And I'm Frodo Baggins," then they introduce the piece, saying something like, "And we'll be performing a scene from *The Lord of the Rings: The Musical,* book and lyrics by Matthew Warchus and Shaun McKenna." Either actor can say that last part, or the actors can say it in unison. Once they have offered the slate, actors should take opening positions and begin their performance.
4. Once the scene is done, the partners may take a bow.
5. Once a team finishes performing, they should put away props and return any furniture to its original positions, restoring the room to pre-performance condition. The professor will identify the next performing team. The new team may set up the space as needed for their scene regarding furniture, props, etc. Once ready, they need to wait until the professor has finished notes for the previous team and gives the signal to begin.
6. Once all groups have performed, it is Circle of Feedback time. Class members need to take careful notes on peers' performances, striving to identify two strengths and two weaknesses for each scene. The class will discuss these identified strengths and weaknesses in the circle.
7. At the end of the Circle of Feedback, the professor will announce the new partners for the next scene, Scene #2. Scene #2 is a scene from a published play identified as a comedy. The running time should be five to seven minutes.

Homework

Each student in the class brings a comedic scene to the next class assemblage. Actors assemble! The professor will work with all teams to help them decide during class which scene, brought by which partner, will be performed by each team.

Lesson 28
Scene #2 Rehearsal

1. Each team member presents the comedic scene the team member brought to class.
2. Once the professor has approved each submitted script, the teams should separate and read each scene aloud.
   A. Once the partners have read both scenes, they will decide which scene to do.
   B. In the event of irreconcilable differences, the professor will decide which scene the team will perform.
3. Each team will read their selected scene aloud for the entire class.
4. Class will discuss the strengths and weaknesses of each team's scene and brainstorm on staging possibilities as appropriate.

Homework

1. Teams need to decide on and design a floor plan. Bring the floor plan to class.
2. Teams need to block their scene. At this point, decide the blocking and record it in pencil next to lines on a copy of the script.

Lesson 29
Day Two
Scene #2 Rehearsal

1. Today is a rehearsal day for Scene #2, the comedy scene. Blocking should be complete, each team should run their scenes as many times as possible during the class time allotted.
2. Each team should consult with the professor for at least one guided run-through. When not working with the professor, teams are free to work as they choose.

Homework

If actors are not off-book yet, memorize, for next rehearsal is off-book and the final rehearsal before performing the scene for a grade.

Lesson 30
Day Three
Scene #2 Rehearsal

1. Today is off-book, final rehearsal for Scene #2.
2. Each team will watch all the other teams perform. Students, take notes and provide feedback when encouraged to do so.
3. Each team will run their scene and receive the professor's feedback.
4. Actors may call for line, but it is not recommended. If an actor wishes to call for line, please identify a classmate to follow on book.

Acting I Final Scene Evaluation

Student Name _____ Grade _____

Character Focus
1   2   3   4   5   6   7   8   9   10

Emotion Action
1   2   3   4   5   6   7   8   9   10

Partner Communication
1   2   3   4   5   6   7   8   9   10

Energy
1   2   3   4   5   6   7   8   9   10

Sense of Urgency
1   2   3   4   5   6   7   8   9   10

Blocking Performance
1   2   3   4   5   6   7   8   9   10

Body Language
1   2   3   4   5   6   7   8   9   10

Line Interpretation
1   2   3   4   5   6   7   8   9   10

Motivation Illustration
1   2   3   4   5   6   7   8   9   10

Tactic Exploration
1   2   3   4   5   6   7   8   9   10

Lesson 31
Final Exam
Scene #2 Performance

1. The professor will call for teams to perform in the order determined by the professor.
2. Once a team is called, they should set up furniture and props as needed for the performance. Once the performance space is ready, they should wait for the professor to tell them to begin.
3. For opening slate, actors should say their names, as in Actor One says, "Hi, I'm Bruce Wayne," then the second actor follows with "And I'm Dick Grayson." Then they introduce the piece, saying something like, "And we'll be performing a scene from *Holy Musical B@tman!* with book by Matt and Nick Lang." Either actor can say that last part or they may say it in unison. Once they have offered the slate, actors can take opening positions and begin the performance.
4. At performance end, the partners can take a bow at center stage. Saying "Thank you" is not necessary but it might be nice. People like it, I think.
5. Once a group has finished their performance, that group needs to restore the room to pre-performance condition. The professor will identify the next group to perform. The new group may set up the space as needed for their scene. Once ready, they should wait until the professor signals to begin.
6. Once all groups have performed, the semester is over. What, that soon? I know, right!

Conclusion

In conclusion, this is the end. Honestly, I feel a little like Deadpool at the end of *Deadpool,* in the after-credit scene when he is doing his Ferris Bueller impersonation. Why are you still here? The book is over, go home. But I do feel that some form of summation is due, which probably goes back to my training in public speaking. Here goes:

I hope you got along well with your classmates this semester, because you may be in future classes or shows with them. You learn more when there is less tension in the room because there are fewer distractions. If you do not hate someone in the room, it is easier to focus on the assignment. The same goes for when you are not wilting beneath the glower of someone else's hate ray. Dame Judi Dench touched on this subject when she discussed how important the closeness of an acting company is, and for this semester that is what you have been, and will be, in any future acting class you take. Inner conflicts within the company or class hurt the art and hobble the learning. Dench (2010) was doing *Macbeth* at a theatre called The Other Place in Stratford-upon-Avon. She said the women were all crammed into one dressing room, the men in another: "But this induced a wonderful company feeling, and an unbelievable air of levity, with lots of stupid schoolboy and schoolgirl jokes. When we actually came to do the play, straight through without an interval, it was a very concentrated piece. That is what creates a company, and an audience will always register if members of a company have a rapport with each other" (77).

Imagine that: loving the people you work with, a goal I highly recommend for an acting class. After all, you are less likely to skip class if you enjoy being there instead of considering it just another session with "those jerks." If you love what you are doing, you become a source of education yourself.

Amy Poehler (2014) states that, "Watching great people do what you love is a good way to start learning how to do it yourself" (109). If you love what you are doing, your classmates can learn from watching you. If they are full of bliss in class, you can learn from watching them. And if your professor enjoys being in the classroom with you, then you all can learn more from the professor. It makes a nice positive pyramid of learning.

Young Frankenstein

Hopefully in future acting classes you will have good professors. Remember, you can learn from anyone, no matter their curriculum vitae or pedigree. Judi Dench (2010) believes that actors need to be taught by teachers who have actually worked in a theatre, because "most people need somebody to tell them what it is actually like to be in a company, how you should behave, and the homework you must do, so that you don't take up a lot of other people's time" (7). Part of what she is referring to is the gap between theory and practice. Some acting programs or classes might be heavy on the art side of acting and neglect the reality of the business side.

I believe acting professors should be confident enough to share their experiences and qualifications with the class. If the professor is not a student's cup of tea, it might be a personality collision, which everyone in a work environment should do their best to avoid. People who let a personal distaste for fellow students or a teacher interfere with their work are standing in the way of their own success. Everyone can learn from anyone. Mindy Kaling (2015) writes that she learned an important lesson about that from writer-producer Greg Daniels:

> You take your mentoring where you can find it, even if it is not being offered to you. Have you ever used your neighbor's Wi-Fi when it wasn't on a password? If you have the opportunity to observe someone at work, you are getting mentoring out of them even if they are unaware or resistant. Make a list of people you think would make the greatest mentors and try to get close enough to steal their Wi-Fi. (89)

But no stalking. You hear that, everybody? No stalking.

Finally—a good word to read in a conclusion—here is a summation of acting points that, should an acting student do them well, will aide them in theatrical auditions.

1. Make sure your objectives and intentions are clear, that your stakes are high, that you have a focused relationship with your imaginary partner, and that your script analysis has given you a fine-grained grasp of the material.

Young Frankenstein

2. Make sure your vocal presence has volume, support, expressiveness, vocal variety, proper pronunciation, and enunciation.
3. Make sure your body language, movement, gestures, and business are fully imagined, carefully planned, and flawlessly executed. Let the movement illustrate the words and ideas of the text.
4. Make sure to take command of the space. Be exuberant and exhilarated. Be focused, relaxed, and filled with glorious purpose.
5. Make sure you have a professional appearance and are well-mannered. Be a positive presence for others.
6. Make sure to remember that you are an actor. And that's pretty cool.

Works Cited

Adler, Stella. *The Art of Acting*. New York, NY: Applause Books, 2000.
Arkin, Alan. *An Improvised Life*. Cambridge, MA: Capo Press Books, 2011.
Baldwin, Alec. *Nevertheless*. New York, NY: HarperCollins, 2017.
Cameron, Kenneth, and Theodore Hoffman. *The Theatrical Response*. London: The Macmillan Company, 1969.
Cohen, Robert. *Acting One, 5th Edition*. Boston, MA: McGraw-Hill, 2008.
Cumming, Alan. *Not My Father's Son*. New York, NY: HarperCollins, 2014.
Dench, Judi, and John Miller. *And Furthermore*. New York, NY: St. Martin's Press, 2010.
Eliot, Marc. *Nicholson*. New York, NY: Crown Archetype, 2013.
Fisher, Carrie. *Wishful Drinking*. New York, NY: Simon & Schuster, 2008.
Kaling, Mindy. *Why Not Me?* New York, NY: Crown Archetype, 2015.
Keaton, Diane. *Then Again*. New York, NY: Random House, 2011.
King, Stephen. *Duma Key*. New York, NY: Scribner, 2008.
Levy, Shawn. *De Niro: A Life*. New York, NY: Crown Archetype, 2014.
Mann, Terrence. *Auditions and Insights with Terrence Mann*. Largo, FL: Jay Gross Studios, 1989.
Moreno, Rita. *Rita Moreno: A Memoir*. New York, NY: Penguin Group, 2013.
Phillips, Pamelia S. "Defining Tone in Singing." Dummies.com. December 19, 2018. https://www.dummies.com/article/academics-the-arts/music/voice/defining-tone-in-singing-179050/.
Poehler, Amy. *Yes Please*. New York, NY: HarperCollins, 2014.
Poitier, Sidney. *The Measure of a Man*. New York, NY: HarperCollins, 2000.
Simkins, Michael. "Method Acting Can Go Too Far—Just Ask Dustin Hoffman." *The Guardian—U.S. Edition*. London: Guardian Media Group, 31 March 2016.
Spacek, Sissy, and Maryanne Vollers. *My Extraordinary Ordinary Life*. New York, NY: Hyperion, 2012.
Union, Gabrielle. *We're Going to Need More Wine*. New York, NY: HarperCollins, 2017.
White, Betty. *If You Ask Me*. New York, NY: G.P. Putnam's Sons, 2011.
Wilder, Gene. *Kiss Me Like a Stranger*. New York, NY: St. Martin's Press, 2005.
Wilson, Edwin. *The Theatre Experience, 13th Edition*. New York, NY: McGraw-Hill Education, 2015.

Index

Absolute Hell (Ackland), 78
"Acting and Reacting" (Mullin), 192
Acting company relationships, 205
Acting One (Cohen), 194
Acting partners, 8, 191, 193
   audience as, 63–64
   working with, 166–167
Action verbs
   blocking and, 176–179
   script analysis, 175–176
   in speeches, 65–66
Actor-audience relationships, 157–158, 159–160
Actor-camera relationship, 158–159
Actor's Nightmare, The (Durang), 109
Adler, Stella, 146
Altman, Robert, 161
Anchor and chain, 142–143
Anxiety, 107
Apologizing, 17
Appearance, 99, 100
Appia, Adolphe, on light and darkness, 90–91
Arkin, Alan, 4, 36, 44, 76, 84, 87, 91, 104, 166
   on educational theatre, 7–8
   on Second City experimentation, 27–28
Articulation, 19
Audiences, 110, 138, 147
   as acting partners, 63–64
   attitudes toward, 96–97
   direct address to, 62–63
   feedback from, 7–8, 23
   first impressions, 12–13
   image of actors, 107–108
   and performances, 159–160

Auditions, auditioning, 57, 64, 94, 104
   arriving for, 98–99
   attitude in, 95–97
   cold-reading, 37–42
   dress for, 100–101
   instructions to, 99–100
   preparation for, 101–103
   techniques in, 97–98
Auditions and Insights with Terence Mann, 121, 185
Aural stimulus, 35

Backstage drama, 75
Backstories, 48
Baldwin, Alec, 3, 70, 82, 84, 103, 121
   on actor-camera relationship, 158–159
Barbecü, Das, 79
Bassett, Angela, 70
Beats, 190
   emotional, 90, 93
   objectives of, 50–51
Beginning (Branagh), 45
Blazing Saddles, 144
Blind casting, 94
Blocking, 52, 53, 102, 108, 168, 171
   action verbs in, 176–179
   changes in, 188–190
   in cold-reading auditions, 40–41
   exercise, 182–184
   monologue, 57–58
   and scene design, 172–173
   and scene goals, 180–181
   in television and movies, 174–175
Blocking plans/schemes, 181–182, 184
Bloody Mama, 4

212 Index

Body, 4, 12, 56, 68, 149
   movements, 64–65, 66, 141
Body language, 20, 41, 59, 65, 145, 207
Bond, James, 97
   casting, 94–95
Brainstorming, 79, 194
   exercises, 80–81
Brando, Marlon, 84, 129
Breathing, 25, 26, 108
Brosnan, Pierce, 97
Burlesque, 137
Bye Bye Birdie, 162

Callbacks, 94, 101–102
Carrie, 77
Casting, 38, 94–95
Castmates, 5
Catch Me If You Can, 49
Cause and effect, 192
Characterization, 19
Characters, 9, 36, 38, 77, 79, 131, 144, 145, 181
   actor intimacy with, 164–165
   backstories of, 48–49
   behavior of, 53–54
   comedy vs. tragedy, 137–138, 139
   development of, 45, 46–47
   goals and aims, 190–191
   objectives, of, 49–50
   reactions of, 191–192
   self-descriptions, 70–71
   visual focus of, 108–109
Cheers, 54
Choreography, 53
   opera vs. musical comedy, 136–137
Circle of attention, 80
Circle of Feedback, 22–23, 118–119, 154, 162
Claremont, Chris, 48
Class etiquette, 75
Coal Miner's Daughter, 67
Cold reading, in auditions, 37–42
Comedy, 147, 148
   anchor in, 142–143
   characters in, 137–138, 145
   exercises, 149–150
   monologues, 120, 151
   plot in, 139–140
   vs. serious plays, 134–135
   Shakespearean, 140–141
Community theatre, 37
Complaints, 76–77
Compliments, 113
Confidence, 99, 109
Conflict, 76
Constructive criticism, 113
Coward, Noel, 45
Craig, Daniel, 94–95, 97
Creativity, and passion, 86
Critical thinking, 69
Cues, in dialogue, 168–170
Cumming, Alan, 7, 76, 106, 110

Dance
   opera vs. musical comedy, 136–137
Daniels, Greg, 206
Dean, Stan, 45, 161
Deception, 77–78
Defiant Ones, The, 45
Del Toro, Benicio, 83
Dench, Judi, 39, 43, 45, 47, 78, 79, 83, 97, 104, 131, 160, 161, 163, 205, 206
   on dedication, 126, 162
DeNiro, Robert, 4, 47, 56, 66, 95, 127
   character preparation, 46, 70
Dialect coaching, 26
Diaphragm, 25, 30
DiCaprio, Leonardo, 49
Dinner with Friends (Margulies), 142
Directability, 99
Directors, 8, 45, 113
   and auditions, 38, 41, 64, 94
   working for, 160–163
Disgraced (Akhtar), 142
Diviners, The (Layman and Leonard), 71–72
Dramatic conflict, 63
Dress, for auditions, 99, 100–101
Duma Key (King), 6

Education, 49
Educational theatre, 7–8, 37
Elfstones of Shannara, The (Brooks), 100
Emotions, 35, 66, 103, 131, 159
   conveying, 32–33, 87–88

motion and, 88–89
visualization of, 89–91
Empathy, 84, 138
Encoding work, 34
English Renaissance, 63
Enunciation work, 31
Evaluations, 21, 42, 116–117, 152–153, 197, 203
Evaluation sheets, 1–2
Evans, Dale, 85
Exercises, 1, 4
acting partner, 166–167
actor-audience relationships, 157–158
actor behavior, 165
blocking, 182–184
body, 149
brainstorming, 194
breathing and speaking, 26
challenges to actors, 132–133
cold-reading, 42
comedic, 149
emotions, 91
encoding work, 34
face, 32, 150
fully engaged speaking, 29–30
group bonding, 10
guided meditation, 92
introduction monologue, 9
meet and greet, 155
off-book rehearsals, 152
physical actions, 92
physical performance, 68
rehearsal, 80–81
stage fright, 106, 111
stimuli reactions, 35–36
vocal, 27, 30–32, 150, 187–188
warm-up, 12–14
winning, 194
word emphasis, 187
Exposition, 62
Eye contact, 62, 161

Face, 20
exercises, 32, 150
Facial expressions/gestures, 20, 33, 39
think-feel-speak, 34–35
Farce, 137
Fear, 107, 108

Feedback, 114, 124–125, 129, 172
audience, 7–8
monologue performance, 22–23, 118–119
rehearsal, 18–20, 116
First impressions, 12–13
Fisher, Carrie, 125
Flick, The (Baker), 44
Focus, 76, 108
Forrest Gump, 128
Fourth wall, 63

Gender identity, 48
Gershwin, George, 120
Gershwin, Ira, 120
Gestures, 20, 33, 61, 102, 108, 145
hand, 59–60
and illusion of the first time, 188–189
Gielgud, John, 39
Gimmicks, 128
Glengarry Glen Ross (Mamet), 79
Grading, 1–2, 115, 122
Gravity, 144–145
Greek plays, 63, 135, 140, 144
Group bonding, 10

Hamlet, comedic scenes in, 140
Hanks, Tom, 128
Hauser, Frank, 162
Henry V, 45
Hoffman, Dustin, 87–88
Homicide Hunter, 84
Humility, 157
Hygiene, personal, 100, 164
Hypokrites, 5

Illusion of the first time, 33, 35, 186, 188
Imitation, 72
Immersion, 4
Improvisation, 76, 102, 190
Inclusionism, 38
Incrementalization, 74
Intelligence, 49
Interaction, 99
personal, 75–76
Interior life/inner life, 77, 81
Interrogator character, 181

Interviews
  audition, 101–102
  with playwrights, 71–72
Intimacy, 178
  of acting space, 163–164
  of actor and character, 164–165

Job interview, 100
Job security, 7

Kaling, Mindy, 7, 59–60, 109, 206
Kardashian, Kim, 60
Keaton, Diane, 24
Kenda, Joe, 84

LaMotta, Jake, 47
Language
  in comedies, 140–141
  dramatic, 143
Laughter on the 23rd Floor (Simon), 45
Legend of Daniel Boone, The, 185
Leonard, Jim, Jr., 72
  The Diviners, 71
Levy, Shawn, 4, 46, 47, 70
Lies, lying, 5
  performance, 77–78
  stage, 6–7
Life-work balance, 130, 131
Light and darkness, 90–91
Line delivery, varying, 187, 190
Listening, 70, 168
  trigger words, 169–170
Live theatre, 85–86
Long, Dayton, 67, 162
Lucas, George, 83, 147
Lynn, Loretta, 67

Macbeth, 70, 140, 160, 205
MacDougall, Duncan, 83
Magic actor theory, 146
Mann, Terence, 121, 185
Marathon Man, 87
Marital status, 48
Matrix, 107
Meditation, 12, 92
Memorization, 18–19, 69, 185
  monologue, 16, 54
  techniques, 74–75
Memory lapse, 109

Method acting/actors, 83, 87–88, 89
Microphones (mics), use of, 28–29
Midsummer Night's Dream, A, 97
Mind-body coordination, 38
Minnelli, Vincente, as director, 162–163
Monologues, 16, 22, 43, 44, 54, 55
  audition, 101, 102
  blocking, 57–58
  choosing, 10–11, 69–70, 103
  comedy, 120, 151
  exercises, 9, 14–15
  movement in, 56–57
  point of address, 61–62
  rehearsal, 17–21, 105
Moreno, Rita, 105
  in *West Side Story,* 164–165
Motivation, 53, 62
Movement, 61, 102, 177
  body, 64–65
  in comedy, 141, 142–143, 145
  hand, 59–60
  purposeful, 58–59
  in serious plays, 143–144
  stage, 56–57, 58
  in television sitcoms, 174–175. See also blocking
Musical comedy, 135, 136–137
Music and Stage Setting (Appia), 91

Narrators, 63
Nice Work If You Can Get It (Gershwin and Gershwin), 120
Nicholson, Jack, 128
  on Vincente Minnelli, 162–163
Non-realistic acting, 150
  in comedies, 135, 137, 139, 143, 149
Nunn, Trevor, 83

Olfactory stimulus, 36
Olivier, Laurence, 87–88
Opening slate, 114
Opera, vs. musical comedy, 135–137
Oral communication, 25
Other Place in Stratford-upon-Avon, The, 205

Panic attacks, 107
Parks and Recreation, 108
Peanuts, 85

Penn, Sean, 83
People watching, 66–67, 68
Person versus nature, 63
Person versus person, 63
Person versus self, 63
Peterman, Donald, 158
Physical actions, 181, 190
  communication with, 32–33
Physicality, warm-up exercises, 14, 114, 116, 118
Playwrights, 8, 48, 175, 177
  meeting/interviewing, 71–72
  respect for, 44–46
Plot
  character objectives in, 49–50
  in comedy, 139–140
Poehler, Amy, 86, 95, 108, 205
Point of address, 26, 61–62
Poitier, Sidney, 8, 45, 73, 86, 87, 129, 192
  on life and personality, 83–84
Posture, 20
  in non-realistic comedy, 144–145
Posture work, 30–31
Presence, 59, 87
Producers, 160–161
Professionalism, 122, 207
  in auditions, 99, 100
Prompting, prompters, 17–18
Pronunciation, 19
Pryor, Richard, 190

Raging Bull, 47, 127
Realism, 79, 135, 145–146, 150
  comedic, 137, 143, 149
Rehearsals, 75, 113, 114, 172
  with acting partners, 167, 168–169
  discipline and, 74, 76
  feedback, 18–20, 116
  monologue, 102, 105
  prompting in, 17–18
  scene, 195–197, 200–201
  and stage fright, 106, 109
Rejection, 103, 108
Repertory company, 5
Repetition, 61, 74, 185, 186
Research, 70–71, 74, 80, 101
  people watching as, 66–67
  role, 46–47

Reviews, 71
Richard III (Shakespeare), 45–46
Rogers, Roy, 85
Roles
  choice of, 69–70
  researching, 46–47

Satire, 137
Scene designers, 51–52, 172–173
Scenes, 50–51, 173, 203
  blocking, 172–174
  environment of, 52–53
  goals of, 180–181
  performance, 198, 204
  rehearsal, 195–197, 200–202
Scripts
  analysis of, 43, 47–53, 175–176, 207
  holding and reading positions, 39–40
  researching, 46–47
  respect for, 44–46
  selecting, 54–55
Sebastian, Laura, 164
Second City, experimentation, 27–28
Self-awareness, 128–129
Self-descriptions, 70–71
Self-knowledge, 128
Sensation stimulus, 36
Serious plays
  vs. comedies, 134, 140–141
  exercises, 149–150
  movement in, 142, 143–144
Set design, 136
Sets, 51–52
Setting sketches, 173–174
Shakespeare, William, 45, 144
  use of comedy, 140–141
Simkins, Michael, 87–88
Singing, 136
Six Degrees of Separation (Guare), 63
Slapstick, 141
Slates, 97, 114
Soliloquies, 61, 62
Solo performance work, 32
Space, 51, 52, 207
  intimacy of, 163–164
  stage, 56, 57
Spacek, Sissy, 4, 67, 75, 77, 83, 85, 105, 123, 130, 159

Spears, Stan, 67
Spurs, 66, 191
Stage business, 64–65, 108, 190
Stage directions, 175
Stage fright, 106, 107, 108, 109, 111, 112
Stage lies, 6–7
Stage movement, 12, 56
   blocking, 57–58
   purposeful, 58–59
Staging of Wagner's Musical Dramas, The (Appia), 91
Stance, 59
Stanislavski, Konstantin, method acting, 89
Strasberg, Lee, 89
Superobjective, 51, 142, 180, 193
Sweat (Nottage), 142

Taxi Driver, 4
Technical acting/actors, 87–88
Theatre Experience, The (Wilson), 137
Theatrical Response, The (Cameron and Hoffman), 146
Think-feel-speak, 33–34
Throat work, 30
Time management
   auditioning, 98–99
   discipline and, 73–74
Tragedy, 139, 141, 142, 148
   characters in, 137–138
   vs. comedy, 134–135, 140
   movement in, 143–144
Treusch, Bill, 105
Trigger words, 191
   in dialogue, 168–170
21 Grams, 83

Union, Gabrielle, 103–104

Verbing, in dialogue 178–180, 191
Vinyl Id, The (Whatley), 65
   trigger words in, 168–169
Visual focus, 61
   concentration on, 108–109
Visualization, of emotional reactions, 89–91
Visual stimulus, 25
Vocal identity, 26, 27, 207
Vocal performance, 19
   varying, 187–188
Vocals, warm-up exercises, 13, 114, 116, 118
Vocal training, 25, 26
Voice, 12, 25, 148, 150
   microphone use, 28–29

Warm-ups, 13, 14, 114, 116, 118
West Side Story, 130
   Rita Moreno and, 164–165
When Harry Met Sally, 180
White, Betty, 112, 122, 168
Wilder, Gene, 5, 8, 89, 100, 190, 192
Wilson, August, 49
Winters, Shelley, 4
Wizard of Oz, The, 53
Work ethic, 75
Working relationships
   with actors, 155–157, 163–164
   with directors, 160–162
Work-life balance, 130, 131
Work of Living Art, The (Appia), 91
Writers. *See* Playwrights

Yeah buts, 77